Endorse
Thoughts from the Mound

For over 26 years I've known Jeff Jenkins. He was 'my preacher' when I was in college. He and his wife, Laura, adopted my future wife and me in the church's college ministry. Later, Jeff led us in premarital counseling. I served as a preaching intern under him. Jeff became a father in the faith to me. When I was a younger preacher I would often seek his advice and today I still do. I'm fortunate to live just down the road from 'the Mound' and very often we meet to talk about the Lord's work. Now, in Jeff's book "More Thoughts From the Mound," you can glean the same wisdom so many of us have sought from him over the years. You'll be richly rewarded from his reflections on life and the truth from God's Word.
Jason Moon,
Preaching Minister, Waterview Church of Christ, Richardson, TX

"More Thoughts from the Mound" is a head-on practical approach to real-life issues. Jeff has a unique ability to provide comfort and encouragement while confronting some of our deepest concerns. This life has no shortage of adversity. Living as a Christian in a fallen world is anything but easy. However, hope is always on the horizon, and Jeff does a masterful job of exposing that hope and directing our focus toward heaven. Jeff is my friend, mentor, and brother in Christ. He is a man who loves God, loves the church, and loves people. This love is illuminated in his writing. I am grateful for men like Jeff A. Jenkins who seek every opportunity to present God's Word in loving compassion.
Chris McCurley,
Preaching Minister, Oldham Lane Church of Christ, Abilene, TX

Preachers hear almost every day, "I just do not have time to read and study my Bible!" Jeff Jenkins has written another book of devotional

thoughts and Biblical lessons that will help you begin to read the Bible daily. These brief yet, meaningful short readings will bless your life and stimulate you to read further in God's Word. I know you will be blessed by getting this book. The only problem is... you will want to read it all in one sitting!
Steve Bailey
Preaching Minister, Brown Street Church of Christ, Waxahachie, Texas

God said of Israel, "My people have forgotten Me, days without number" (Jer. 2:32). How could something like this happen with self-proclaimed "people of God"? While there may be many reasons, one rises to the top: The people had no proactive plan to remember God or to think about His Word. In this book "More Thoughts From the Mound," Jeff is helping us be proactive in remembering God. In this easy-to-read book, Jeff brings together humor, story-telling, illustrations and dozens of biblically based observations. Everyone, from the new Christian to the seasoned veteran, will benefit from this work.
Denny Petrillo,
Director, Bear Valley School of Preaching, Denver, Colorado

This book is excellent for the encouragement of God's people to be spiritually healthy by feeding on God's word daily, and I know of no better person to write such a book than my brother Jeff.
Gary Bradley,
Huntsville, AL

Jeff Jenkins has blest us by producing fifty-two essays to lift our spirits, comfort our hearts, and strengthen our commitment to the Bible as the authoritative word of God. In "More Thoughts from the Mound," the author provides devotional meditations that will help provide guidance, perspective, and hope for our own lives and for the lives of those around us. When Jeff Jenkins speaks or writes, we need to listen because we can be confident that his message is grounded in the Scriptures and applicable for life in the real world.
Howard W. Norton
Elder, College Church of Christ, Searcy, AR

In a time when the church of our Lord seems under attack, we need heroes of the faith to powerfully remind us of their love for Jesus Christ and His church. In his wonderful book, Jeff Jenkins profoundly fulfills that need, as we hear the voice and see the heart of a servant leader who cherishes the bride of Christ. With each chapter, Jeff guides us through the minefields of life while also showing us the path to safety found only in the arms of Jesus. Each word is challenging, yet also convicting. Jeff writes as one with authority, and we're blessed to listen.
Jacob D. Hawk
Preaching Minister, Faith Village Church of Christ, Wichita Falls, TX

In contrast to the challenges and struggles of this world, More Thoughts From the Mound echoes the tones of reassurance and peace one can enjoy when living according to God's plan. In his latest book, Jeff constructs an experience-filled, encouraging read for all Christians seeking to serve through proclaiming the love of Christ.
Scott E. Latham
Elder, University Church of Christ, Montgomery, AL

"More Thoughts from the Mound," a second volume of fifty-two devotional messages, will encourage and inspire you to be stronger in your faith and more faithful in your service to the Lord. I love this book because I know and love its author as a man who is pure in heart. Jeff Jenkins writes from a mind and a ministry that struggles with life's greatest questions, provides the Bible's greatest answers, and applies those answers to living the greatest life, the one completely devoted to God.
Billy R. Smith
Dean, College of Biblical Studies
Freed-Hardeman University, Henderson, TN

More Thoughts from the Mound

Jeff A. Jenkins

© 2016 The Jenkins Institute

All rights reserved.

ISBN-13: 978-1541056145
ISBN-10: 1541056140

Published by The Jenkins Institute

thejenkinsinstitute.com

Editing: Diana Kinser
Cover design: Chad Landman
Interior layout: Joey Sparks

This volume is gratefully dedicated to friends around the world who have been a wonderful source of encouragement in the writing of these "Thoughts..."

May God continue to bless you as you grow closer to Him each day and as you seek to glorify Him.

Acknowledgements

"More Thoughts from the Mound" would have never been written or published had it not been for "Thoughts from the Mound." I am indebted to my adopted son, Michael Whitworth for publishing "Thoughts from the Mound" as a gift to us.

For nearly twenty-five years Jay Lockhart has been a wonderful co-worker, a dear friend, and a trusted confidant. His writing the foreword for this book means more to me than he can know. Thank you Jay! Just like you, your words are kind and gracious.

Thanks to Joey Sparks for all he does for The Jenkins Institute. Joey is our outstanding editor, lay-out guru, and all around go-to guy for most everything we do. Joey, we can't thank you enough for your willingness to share your giftedness with us.

My special gratitude to Diana Kinser, our friend and sister in Christ, for proofing this book. Diana, you made this book better than it would have been. We love you and Clay.

Chad Landman designed the cover for the first "Thoughts" book and we are grateful to him for designing the cover for this book as well. Chad, you are a true servant.

We want to express our deep appreciation to our Lewisville Church family. Thank you for allowing us to be a part of your lives. You are one of God's greatest blessings to us. Thank you for allowing me to share the stories found in this book as well as many more like them through the years, and thank you for sharing with us your story. We love you dearly.

Without the readers of our blog, our posts, and our books, this volume would not be possible. Thank you for your constant kind words of encouragement. Thank you for continuing to read what we write. Our sincere prayer is that you are blessed by this book.

Last, but certainly not least, thank you to my wonderful wife. Laura, my life would be empty without you. Thank you for supporting me in every work and for putting up with me. You are the best wife and the best friend any man could ever have. ILYFAF!

Contents

Foreword	ixx
Introduction	xxi
What on Earth Are We Doing and Where Is God?	1
The Bible Contains the Mind of God	7
Sunday	11
Never Forget	17
Embarrassed and Ashamed	23
Conflict Management in the Family	27
Brothers, We Should Pray Before We Preach	33
Is Everything Perfect?	37
He Looked Too Much Like Jesus	39
Don't Let Them Take Away Your Faith	43
How Will You Preach This Sunday?	49

Impressive or Impressed?	53
What I Want to Tell Them	57
"My Pleasure"	61
Preachers...It Matters	65
You're a Real Man Now!	69
"That God Thing"	73
Stay Focused	77
Is Preaching Important?	81
Preachers Need Passion	85
What Are You Preaching Sunday?	89
A Special Cup of Coffee	95
Five Suggestions for Working with Difficult People	97
Remember	101
A Birthday Thought	105
Our God Can, Our God Will	111
Are You Growing in Your Faith?	115
Do You Want to Keep Your Preacher?	119
Wisdom from 7 Eleven	125

My Father's Writing	129
We've Got to Do This Quickly	133
"I Will Never Be Lost!"	137
"Why Am I Here?"	141
Is This the Place?	145
Redeeming Value???	149
Not Your Normal Happy Self	155
"Are You Ready for Sunday?"	159
You Just Never Know	163
Stir What You Got!	167
The Land of the Living	171
Eating with Impunity	175
Immersed in the Word	179
The People Are Suffering	183
A Late Night Prayer	187
Can't Get the Hang of It	191
Anonymous	195
Everybody's a Role Model	199

A Lifetime of Lessons   203

A Beige Life   207

I Ain't Gonna Do It   209

May I Help You?   213

Stick to What You Know, Pops   217

Foreword

Jeff Jenkins has been preaching the gospel for thirty-seven years. I have known Jeff for twenty-five of those years, and I have found him to be a great preacher, a biblical preacher, a true man of God, and a trusted and faithful friend. He loves God and the Lord Jesus Christ; he loves the church; he loves his family; he loves preachers; and he loves preaching. Jeff's love for preachers has been seen through the years as he has been the mentor of many young preachers and the friend of all. I know of no one who is more highly respected as a builder of local churches and a lover of the brotherhood than is Jeff. He comes from a rich heritage and a family of preachers.

Out of this background, Jeff has written two books: "Thoughts From the Mound" and "God's Plan for Unity." With his brother, Dale, he has written "Don't Quit On Monday" and "A Father's Heart." Jeff has also written single chapters in a number of helpful books edited by others. Whatever Jeff writes proves to be a blessing to his readers. This book will be no exception. It is biblically sound, compassionately written, and practical in nature. The current volume covers a variety of thought provoking material. Jeff writes about God, worship, family, courage, memory, conflict, prayer, suffering, preaching, faith, communication, and other important topics with skill, understanding, and passion. The book is written with a gifted writer's ingenuity and is divided into more than fifty brief and challenging sections. So, may I encourage you to read on and receive a blessing.

Jay Lockhart
Whitehouse, TX

Introduction

The book you are about to read is not a theological treatise. It is not a doctrinal discourse. This book is a collection of fifty-two blog posts and articles written over about a five-year span of time.

These devotional "Thoughts" are intended to encourage people to grow closer to God, to help us in strengthening our faith, and to bring peace when we have troubled hearts.

Some of these "Thoughts" are written specifically to preachers. Encouraging preachers is a passion that floods my heart. I am committed to spending whatever years God allows me to have left on this earth, in encouraging men who have dedicated their life to the preaching of the Gospel. If you are not a preacher, some of these thoughts will not mean as much to you. Feel free to read them anyway, and please share them with a preacher you know who might benefit from them.

Nearly all of these articles are about real life situations and real people. Some of these people are very close friends of ours. Some have been friends in the past. Some of these "Thoughts" are about folks we have met only once, but in a short time they made a strong impression on us.

All of these "Thoughts" were written while we have lived in Flower Mound, Texas. We love our home town and feel blessed to live here. The people are warm, friendly, and caring. My sincere prayer is that "More Thoughts from the Mound" will encourage you to be closer to the Lord. Thank you for taking the time to read these "Thoughts" from my heart.

Jeff A. Jenkins
Flower Mound, TX
December, 2016

What on Earth Are We Doing and Where Is God?

Why is there so much violence in our world? Why do we have to see wickedness, sin, and destruction? It seems like there is strife and contention all around us. Doesn't anybody care about laws anymore? And what about justice in our world? It seems like justice is not upheld but rather is perverted. Why does it seem like wickedness is winning???

Questions like these are in the conscience of our nation. The blogosphere, Twitter, Facebook, podcasts, and all the news are saturated with these very thoughts. However, the questions raised here are not from the news or a blog. They were asked by one of God's men more than 2500 years ago.

When you read these words from Habakkuk you would think that he's been reading our mail (or our blogs, or our news)! You would think he is writing about modern day America. Like many today, this man of God is crying out to the heavens, "Do You hear my prayers, why won't You answer?" He wonders aloud if God knows what is going on in the world. He wonders if God cares, and he cries to God, "Why aren't You doing something about this mess?"

What is the violence, wickedness, sin, destruction, strife, contention, disobedience, and injustice he is concerned so much about? Could the injustice be some form of class or racial injustice? Could the strife be racial tension? Could the violence be from people taking the law into their own hand? Could it be people rioting in the streets because they feel they aren't being heard? Could the sin he mentions here be when people break the laws of God and rewrite what He has said or simply claim that it doesn't apply to them? Could his statement about wickedness winning be based upon the feeling that his world had relegated God and His Word to a bit player on the world stage?

There is much about what was going on in Habakkuk's world that we cannot be certain about. There is much about what is taking place in our world that we can't understand, comprehend, or figure out. Our collective hearts are broken, our nation is troubled, and we are hurting. So, what do we do? Like God's man from long ago, we cry out to our Father, we seek His help, His guidance, and His answers. We wonder if there is anything we can do and should be doing.

Many believe that the answer to this is simply dialogue. Let's talk about it. Let's talk about the racial problems in our world. Let's discuss injustices. Let's get together and discuss what we should do about Church issues (fill in the blank here with numerous concerns). Let's have a conversation.

This may be a great starting point. One thing we can know for certain is that trying to hide under a rock and act like these problems don't exist will not make them go away. It doesn't help to refuse to talk. So, let's talk. Let's have conversations. But let's be sure that we are not naive enough to think that our conversations are going to cure the world's ills. Let's not think that if we can just get together and discuss problems in the Church that we will fix them!

The most basic reason that this alone will not work is because we are humans. We come to the table with preconceived ideas and answers. Each of us believes that we know what is needed. But we should not allow that to deter us. We can work diligently to make the world around us a better place. Let's do something, anything! Let's work to find solutions and then let's work the solutions!

And DO the right thing. Another man of God said, "Mankind, He has told you what is good and what it is the LORD requires of you: to act justly, to love faithfulness, and to walk humbly with your God" (Micah 6:8). Did you catch that? "Act justly," do what is right. Don't just talk about doing right; act on what you know.

Let's just be real honest for a moment. The truth is we can't fix this world. We can't solve the problems. We can't correct injustice. We can't end violence. We can't stop people who choose to ignore the Word of God. We can't make people do the right thing! Not the government, not the media, not preachers, not the Church, not any of us, or all of us!

We are helpless, hopeless and useless without Jesus. All the conferences, conversations, plans, programs, agendas, money, ideologies, work, religious activity, and the collective wisdom in the entire world is meaningless if we don't bring Christ, as well as His Word, to the table. Jesus is the only answer. The Good News about Him will make a difference.

The best thing we can do for our world is to keep sharing the Gospel. Keep showing what it means to have the Prince of Peace in our lives by what we do for others. Keep glorifying God by the way we live. Keep praying that our world will turn to Him. Keep allowing our hearts to be permeated with kindness, love, and compassion for every person.

And one more thought. Above all, above all, don't give up on God! Remember Habakkuk? God did hear His cries. God was looking down on the world, and He was very aware of what was going on. God was doing something.

Listen to His words: "Look among the nations! Observe! Be astonished! Wonder! Because I am doing something in your days— You would not believe if you were told" (Habakkuk 1:5).

We have no idea what God is doing in our nation, in our world, and in the Church. He may well be working in our lives. He may be working in you to make a difference in the world or the life of the Church. He may be raising up someone or many "someones" right now who will be strong enough and brave enough to be used for His glory.

So, don't give up on God. Keep praying. Keep crying out to Him. Keep talking. Keep sharing the Good News with others. Keep doing the right thing. Keep trusting in our Lord.

Dear God, please help us to learn to do the right thing. Help us learn to not only listen to You, but to rely upon You, and to follow Your Word. We thank you, dear Father, that You have not left us alone in this world. In the Name of our Loving Savior we pray, Amen.

The Bible Contains the Mind of God

My Dad was a man of relatively few words. Even though preaching was his vocation, he seemed always to choose his words carefully. He specifically was not real big on trivial talk. When he did say something, it always seemed appropriate, beneficial, and worthwhile.

Our good friend Daniel Courington, who worked with Dad during the last years of Dad's life, sent this note to us shortly after Dad passed away: "Last words ever written by Brother Jerry in the Roebuck Reminder: (the Church bulletin) 'for the Bible contains the mind of God.'"

Reading those words was a wonderful blessing to my life then, and it still is today. It reminded me of how meaningful Dad's words always were. It reminded me of the need to be more serious about my preaching and teaching. It reminded me of the awesomeness of what those of us who preach are privileged to do. It reminded me of the wonderful gift that has been given to us to proclaim the unsearchable riches of Christ.

Preaching is one of God's chosen methods of letting people everywhere in the world know His mind. "For the word of the cross is foolishness to those who are perishing, but to us who are being saved it is the power of God. For it is written, 'I will destroy the wisdom of the wise, And the cleverness of the clever I will set aside.' Where is the wise man? Where is the scribe? Where is the debater of this age? Has not God made foolish the wisdom of the world? For since in the wisdom of God the world through its wisdom did not come to know God, God was well-pleased through the foolishness of the message preached to save those who believe" (1 Corinthians 1:18-21). Those of us who preach and teach God's Word must never forget this. When we preach, we are being used by God to help reveal His mind.

Not because God pours it miraculously into our brains, but because we are equipped through our study of the Bible to help people understand the mind of God to the degree that He has revealed it. "They read from the book, from the law of God, translating to give the sense so that they understood the reading" (Nehemiah 8:8).

Because of this, it is infinitely more important that we preach the Word of God, the Bible (2 Timothy 4:1-4), than it is for us to give a commentary on the news, to spend too much time in other literary sources, or to perform a stand-up routine.

We need to reveal the mind of God as it pertains to our daily lives. Thank God He has not left us alone in this world. He has given us help for every aspect of our life and a roadmap that will not lead us down a wrong path.

We need to reveal the mind of God concerning our families. The world, our government, and the entertainment industry have definite ideas about the family. They have made their ideas clear. The only way our families can be truly happy and fulfilled is when we follow the mind of God.

Only in the Bible can we learn the best tools for how we should treat our mates, how we should raise our children, and how we should love one another in our families.

We need to reveal the mind of God about His Church. There have been thousands of books written and seminars conducted to tell us how we need to "do" church. These are all fine, if they are in tune with God's Word. In the Bible, we learn from the mind of God how He wants us to worship, how He wants His Church to evangelize, how He wants His Church to be organized, and how He wants us to treat one another. How badly we need to learn the mind of God as we relate to one another in the life of His Church.

We need to reveal the mind of God about how He feels about our fellow man. The Word of God tells us how God feels about the people around us (John 3:16; Romans 5:8). One of our great responsibilities as preachers is to teach and show those who listen to us how we are to be kind, loving, caring, and forgiving to those around us.

Some might say it is arrogant to claim to speak the mind of God. My thought would be that it is much more arrogant to stand and speak our own mind. Wouldn't we much rather speak the Word of God than our own words? We really do have a treasure, and we should feel humbled that God has chosen to reveal His mind through us simple jars of clay (2 Corinthians 4:7).

Dear Father in Heaven, we thank You for revealing Yourself to us in Your Word. We pray that we will do our part to make Your Name known among all the nations. We pray that more and more will turn to You. Help us to love You more each day. In Jesus Name we pray, Amen.

Sunday

On Sunday, by the power of God, Jesus burst forth from the grave.

On Sunday, the Holy Spirit showed His great power by indwelling the Apostles in Jerusalem.

On Sunday, people from everywhere gathered to hear the Word of the Lord.

On Sunday, Peter preached a powerful, convicting sermon.

On Sunday, thousands were baptized into Christ for the forgiveness of their sins.

On Sunday, God began a movement that would forever change and impact the world like no other movement in the history of mankind.

On Sunday, people will gather together in homes, in rented buildings, on ships, and in large facilities to worship our Creator.

On Sunday, all over the world, our risen Lord and King will be remembered through the observance of His Supper.

On Sunday, we will do our best to offer up prayers that will be a pleasing aroma to our loving Father.

On Sunday, we will seek to praise Him by singing from the depths of our hearts.

On Sunday, we will return to Him the first fruits of all that He has so bountifully showered upon us.

On Sunday, Christians around the world will listen as His marvelous Word will be read and heralded by preachers of the Gospel.

On Sunday, people who are hurting physically, emotionally, and spiritually will come together to be encouraged, edified, and strengthened by binding their hearts together with others who are hurting.

On Sunday, single moms will spend time getting their children ready to gather with others in worship.

On Sunday, an elderly person will attend their first worship without their departed loved one who they have faithfully sat beside for more than fifty years.

On Sunday, a teenager will be present to worship without anyone in their family because a friend invited them to worship.

On Sunday, parents will sit in places of worship praying that a child who has walked away from the Lord will find their way back to Him.

On Sunday, a Christian couple will sit beside one another during worship wondering if their marriage is going to make it.

On Sunday, a godly Christian woman will sit in worship praying that her husband will obey Jesus.

On Sunday, there will be people who are present in worship physically but their minds and hearts will be a million miles away.

On Sunday, concerned members of congregations will do everything within their power and will pray with all they have in them that the Church will not divide.

On Sunday, shepherds in God's Church will be present for worship and will be praying fervently that they are doing their best to shepherd and feed the flock that He has entrusted to them.

On Sunday, elders will be praying that their preacher will proclaim the life-changing Word of God with passion and conviction.

On Sunday, a preacher will stand before the Church with his heart breaking because of family concerns.

On Sunday, a preacher will stand to preach worn out physically and emotionally, knowing he is underprepared because of spending so much time ministering to people.

On Sunday, a preacher will stand to proclaim God's Word with a heavy heart because of disagreements with Church leadership and wondering if he will have a job on Monday.

On Sunday, a preacher will stand before the people of God and preach his heart out, praying all the time that it will make a difference in the lives of those who listen.

On Sunday, there will be rejoicing in Heaven and on earth when someone gives their life to Christ by being baptized for the forgiveness of sins.

On Sunday, prayers will be answered when a prodigal makes their way home.

On Sunday, God will be pleased when His children worship Him in spirit and in truth with all their hearts.

Dear Father, help us on Sunday to pour out ourselves to You. We pray that You will be pleased with everything that we do as we gather together to worship. As we seek to glorify You and honor our Savior we pray that our hearts will be right. In Jesus' name we pray, Amen.

Never Forget

First of all, let me be clear. I have never fought in a war, lived through the depression, had my home blown away by a tornado or a hurricane, or been fired from a job (at least not so far!), but my family has experienced some difficult days in our lives.

Each of these days is memorable for different reasons, and we are convinced that marvelous lessons have been learned in each of those difficult days.

I remember vividly as a young boy attending my grandfather's funeral. To me, Paw-Paw was bigger than life.

We remember the day we lost a son. It was the saddest and most difficult day of my life to that point. Even though it's been more than thirty years ago, it still hurts when we think about it.

We remember the day we learned that my wife Laura had cancer. It was devastating to hear those words from the doctor that first time.

We remember the day we learned that Laura's cancer had returned nearly ten years after the first battle. During those two difficult periods of our life we learned much about faith and about prayer. We were strengthened and encouraged greatly by our families as well as by the people of God. We praise God that she has been in remission now for ten years!

We remember the night we received word that my mom had passed away. We knew that she had been ill, but we did not expect her to go when she did. We will forever be thankful for the way she poured her life into ours, and how she stood beside my dad for nearly 50 years.

We remember those weeks spent with Dad before he passed away. I remember the moment we knew he wasn't going to make it. We remember the terrible feeling of knowing that the man we respected and loved more than life itself was no longer going to be with us. As so many of you who have experienced losing your parents will understand, it hurts deeply to this day.

Even though it has been more than 20 years ago, we vividly remember April 19, 1995. It was a beautiful Wednesday morning in Oklahoma City. The weather was picture perfect. I had arrived at my office early that morning to spend some time studying before making some visits.

Shortly before 9:00 A.M. I was on the phone with my friend, Gary Bradley in Huntsville, Alabama. We were talking about our families, about enjoyable times we had shared in the past, and about an upcoming seminar.

At 9:02 there was a noise that sounded familiar. Gary heard the noise over the phone from 700 miles away! He asked me what the noise was, and I told him it was probably one of the units in our building kicking on.

Our call was interrupted when one of our secretaries knocked on my door and reported that there had been an explosion downtown.

We turned on a TV and saw the devastating pictures of the Murrah Federal Building shortly after the bombing. We were ten miles away, and we heard the blast! It was later reported that people heard or felt that blast from up to 55 miles away.

That moment, 9:02 a.m., changed the lives of people around the world forever. There were 168 people killed (from a three-month old baby to a 74-year-old), more than 680 others injured, and thousands of lives directly touched by this horrible event. There were numerous lessons we learned from that day.

We saw man at his worst. The people who committed this terrible crime spent years planning this act of hatred. They intentionally took the lives of many children. There are few things we can think of that are worse than hurting children.

We saw man at his best. We watched people volunteer and risk their own lives to attempt to save others. We saw people put their lives on hold to reach out to those who were hurting. We saw a nation of people offer support, prayers, and strength.

We saw the heart of community. The people of Oklahoma City, the state of Oklahoma, and the nation came together to help one another during this terrible crisis. People gave of their time, their money, their resources, and their lives. People everywhere prayed for those whose lives were forever changed by this tragedy.

We saw the meaning of forgiveness. As long as I live, I will never forget hearing a wonderful Christian woman respond to a reporter who asked her, "How can you not have hatred in your heart for those who have done this to you?"

Susan Walton, who endured numerous surgeries due to injuries she received in the bombing, responded by saying, "You can't go to Heaven if you have hatred in your heart!!!" That is what it means to have the mind of Christ (Philippians 2:5).

We saw the church at its best. More than one million dollars poured in from members of the church around the country. Many churches held special prayer services for the victims and families. Churches called asking what supplies were needed and what other ways they could help.

That day stands out in my mind as a day that will never be forgotten. I vividly remember speaking at length with a sweet woman who lost two of her grandchildren in the bombing. She was hurting and the pain on her face was difficult to watch. We prayed together that day, and we've prayed for her numerous times through the years.

Those who have endured this kind of pain understand that one ever fully gets over losing loved ones like this. There are many people who continue to suffer physically and emotionally because of that tragedy.

We also understand more than ever that God is good. He will help us pick up our lives and live them out in His service for His glory.

Dear Father, Help us to never forget Your goodness toward us. Help us never forget the kindness that has been shown to us through others. Help us to show Your love to everyone around us. In the Name of Jesus we pray, Amen.

Embarrassed and Ashamed

That would be me. I'm embarrassed and ashamed of myself. Allow me to explain. It was a red-eye flight by accident. I thought I was booking a 12:20 p.m. flight home from Los Angeles to arrive at 5:20 p.m., just in time to make it to our Monday night Bible study.

The only problem was I booked a 12:20 AM flight that would not arrive home until 5:20 AM! One of my young preacher friends would tell me that at my age it would probably be a good idea to get someone to help me with my scheduling. It had already been a long busy week of speaking and meetings. Now with the prospect of arriving home after no sleep, my attitude was less than stellar.

However, the misstep in scheduling is not the cause of my being embarrassed and ashamed. There was a lady seated next to me on the plane, and not once did I engage her in conversation about Jesus or His Church. As a matter of fact, I barely spoke to her.

It would be nice and comforting if I could blame it on being tired or being upset about the all-night flight. But honestly that is not the only reason for my lack of speaking about the Lord.

Okay, here is my confession of weakness. She didn't smell good. She was a different nationality. She spoke broken English. She wasn't attractive, and to top it all off she was from a different generation (yeah, that one).

My plan whenever I get on a plane is always to say something about Jesus and about the Church. But this time I didn't. I wasn't acting at all like a preacher of the Good News. More importantly, I wasn't at all acting like a Christian who cares about others. And because of that I'm embarrassed and ashamed of myself.

My sincere prayer is that God will forgive me for wasting this opportunity He gave me to tell someone about Jesus.

My prayer for every disciple of Jesus is that we will never again refuse to speak about the love of Christ to everyone we meet.

My prayer is that we will never again judge another person's right to hear about Jesus based on the color of their skin, their level of education, their nationality, their gender, their age, or anything else.

My prayer is that we will realize that every person is created in the image of God.

My prayer is that we will see every person as a soul who desperately needs the Lord.

My prayer is that we will look at every opportunity to tell someone the Good News as a gift from God.

My prayer is that we will show the love of Jesus in the way we treat everyone we meet.

My prayer is that our eyes will be opened and our ears attuned for more opportunities to share the Gospel.

My prayer is that we will consider the fact that every person deserves to hear the Gospel once before any person deserves to hear it twice.

Dear God, please forgive us for the times we have wasted opportunities that You have placed in our path. Please help us to always say something good about Jesus and something good for Jesus to everyone we meet. Dear Father, help us to see every person as someone who is made in Your image. Help us to love the people in our world with the love of Jesus. In His Precious name we pray, Amen.

Conflict Management in the Family

The question is not, "Will conflict occur in our family?" The real questions are, "Will we acknowledge that there is conflict?" "How long will we allow conflict to go on unchecked?" "Will we do anything to help alleviate conflict when it is present?" "What will we do to avoid more conflict in the future?"

There has been conflict in every home since God created the family. The Sacred text informs us of Cain's anger and jealousy toward his brother (Genesis 4:5-8).

Conflict exists because sin is ever present in our world. Families are composed of human beings, and because all human beings sin, (Romans 3:9-10, 23) there will always be conflict in our homes. In addition, because we each have conflict in our own hearts and lives, (Romans 7:15-25) we will have conflict with others.

The question is, "How can we manage conflict in our home?" We will attempt to answer this important question based upon scripture, personal experience, and insight from what others say.

ACKNOWLEDGE THAT CONFLICT EXISTS.

One of the reasons that so many people cannot seem to resolve conflict is because they ignore it. The old adage that says if we ignore something long enough it will go away will not work in making our families better and stronger. We can attempt to hide our heads under a rock, but conflict will remain.

The reason there will always be conflict in families is because families are made up of human beings. Because we all sin (Romans 3:23) and because there are no perfect human beings, conflict will exist. The first step in dealing with conflict is to acknowledge that it does exist.

ACKNOWLEDGE THAT I AM PART OF THE PROBLEM. One of our favorite indoor sports in families is what has been called, "The Blame Game." If I can just find someone else to blame for the conflict, then it doesn't seem so bad. Many people blame their parents for conflicts in their own marriages and families. If my parents had not fought so much, if my parents would have been more attentive, if my parents would have paid more attention to me, I would not be struggling with this.

Others place the blame on everyone else in the family. "My mate is always complaining, always negative, doesn't pay me enough attention, is only concerned with his or her job." All these statements may be true; however it is of great importance that we examine our own lives (2 Corinthians 13:5) to make sure we are not the primary cause of conflict.

ACKNOWLEDGE THAT WE CANNOT RESOLVE ALL CONFLICT WITHOUT HELP.

Ask God to help us. We should never attempt to resolve conflict without asking the Lord to help us. Peter admonishes us to cast all our anxieties on the Lord because He cares for us (1 Peter 5:8). Everyone who has ever dealt with conflict in their family recognizes how much anxiety there is because of the conflict.

God wants to help us. He challenges us to bring our problems to His throne with confidence. "Let us draw near with confidence to the throne of grace, so that we may receive mercy and find grace to help in time of need" (Hebrews 4:16).

If necessary, ask for help from a counselor. There are many Christians who shy away from talking to professional counselors or preachers/elders because they believe it shows a sign of weakness not to be able to resolve their problems on their own.

There are counselors who have a world view that is compatible with Christians. Their counseling is rooted in Scripture and they believe that God's Word provides the answers to every problem.

Spend some time with older couples who have experienced life. These are certainly not people who are perfect. The best models would not claim perfection; nor would they claim they have all the answers. However, we can learn so much from those who have encountered life and worked to keep their marriage together. It is helpful to listen and learn from others who have dealt with difficulties in life.

Find other resources. There are many good books, videos, and audio resources that can be helpful. We would do well to read, watch, and listen to some of these to learn about ways that we can handle conflicts in our families. There are seminars and classes that would be helpful as well. We should avail ourselves of every possible means to help us deal with conflict.

ACKNOWLEDGE THAT CONFLICT IS AN OPPORTUNITY FOR GROWTH. The Word of God makes it clear that when we endure struggles and trials in this life they provide for us opportunities to grow. "Consider it all joy, my brethren, when you encounter various trials, knowing that the testing of your faith produces endurance. And let endurance have its perfect result, so that you may be perfect and complete, lacking in nothing" (James 1:2-4).

It has been well said that every trial we face will either make us bitter or better. It all depends on how we respond when we face conflict in our family. Will we grow in our relationships? Will we become stronger in our faith? There are some steps we can take to ensure that our conflicts become a time of growth.

Understand the problem. Have you ever been involved in an argument with someone, and then you realize you are not sure you know what you are arguing about? A wise man once wrote, "The mind of the intelligent seeks knowledge, but the mouth of a fool feeds on folly" (Proverbs 15:14).

Avoid key words. Through the years as we have counseled many families who are struggling with conflict, we have heard people employ phrases that are of no value to solving the problem. We should avoid using phrases such as, "You never do this or that," and "You always do this or that."

Don't criticize feelings. Feelings are neither right or wrong. They are just feelings. It is unwise, and probably not helpful, to tell someone they should or should not feel a certain way. We cannot command a feeling that someone has in their heart.

Feel the pain of others who are involved in the conflict. When someone in your family is hurting, do you hurt with them? Can you sympathize with what your loved one is going through when there is conflict?

When our brother Peter was discussing how we should live godly lives in our family, he said, "To sum up, all of you be harmonious, sympathetic, brotherly, kindhearted, and humble in spirit." (1 Peter 3:8)

Make things right between those who are in conflict. When we are dealing with conflict we should ask if we can develop a specific plan to make everything right. The Apostle Paul gives us a tremendous plan that we can use to make things right when we are dealing with conflict. "Be of the same mind toward one another; do not be haughty in mind, but associate with the lowly. Do not be wise in your own estimation. Never pay back evil for evil to anyone. Respect what is right in the sight of all men. If possible, so far as it depends on you, be at peace with all men. Never take your own revenge, beloved, but leave room for the wrath of God, for it is written, 'Vengeance is Mine, I will repay,' says the Lord. 'But if your enemy is hungry, feed him, and if he is thirsty, give him a drink; for in so doing you will heap burning coals on his head.' Do not be overcome by evil, but overcome evil with good" (Romans 12:16-21).

Brothers, We Should Pray Before We Preach

As preachers, we are often called upon to pray for people during the most difficult days of their lives. Maybe you've been called upon to pray before a high school ball game, a special ceremony in your area, or even in the halls of some government meeting.

We always consider it an honor when we are asked to pray for others. But what about our prayers that are not a part of our "assigned" work? What about our personal prayer life?

It seems that one of the most crucial times in which we should offer up prayers and requests to God is before we preach. Do you talk to God before you talk to others? May I encourage you to pray today about tomorrow?

Pray that God's Word will change hearts and lives. May we never forget that the power is not in our abilities, our knowledge, or our charisma. The power is always and only in God's life-changing Good News (Romans 1:15-16).

Pray that God's people will be strengthened in their life of faith. We gather with the people of God to edify and encourage. When God's Word is taught God's people will grow (Romans 10:17). The meat of God's Word will help Christians mature and be prepared to face the world on Monday (Hebrews 5:12-6:1).

Pray that you will be able to get yourself out of the way, and let God work. As accomplished as the great Apostle Paul was in his work for the Lord, he still lived with the realization that it was God who should receive all the glory (Galatians 6:14).

If we ever start believing that we are responsible for good results from the work we do, we are in real trouble. "For it is God who is at work in you, both to will and to work for His good pleasure" (Philippians 2:13).

Pray that everyone present (including yourself) can block out the cares of the world for a brief time and be transported before the throne of God to bring proper glory to Him. We desperately need this time each week as God's family to gather around His throne.

In a world that is filled with chaos and confusion, we all need some calm and clarity.

In a world that is filled with bad news, we need the Good News.

In a world where people are hurting, we need some healing.

In a world that is filled with war, we need some peace.

In a world that is filled with hate, we need some love.

In a world that is filled with injustice, we need some of God's justice.

In a world that is filled with death, we need to learn about life.

Pray that God's people will stop fighting with one another and focus on Him. When we focus our hearts and minds on our Lord by praying, praising, and listening to Him, our disagreements have a way of taking care of themselves.

Let's pray that God's people can come together in unity and forget about our differences as we approach the throne of the Almighty. Let's pray that the cross of our Savior can bring peace to our troubled hearts.

Pray that everyone present will leave our time together in worship with a renewed commitment to be the kind of Christians He wants us to be. Pray that God will help us do our part as we proclaim His Word to encourage people to live for Jesus every day.

Pray that our worship will cause people to want to be better husbands, wives, children, neighbors, workers, citizens, and followers of Jesus.

One more thought. Let's all pray for one another. Pray for our brothers who will be standing beneath the cross of Jesus to proclaim the unsearchable riches of Christ. Pray that we will preach with passion as a dying man speaking to dying men.

Dear Father, we thank You for every opportunity we have to preach Your Word. Help us to seek to glorify You in our preaching as well as in our lives. We pray for every man who will stand to proclaim the glorious Gospel. We pray for everyone who will listen to Your Word proclaimed, that lives will be changed and that Your Kingdom will be strengthened. We pray in the name of our Savior, Amen.

Is Everything Perfect?

It happened again the other day. This time Laura and I were sitting in a local cafe when the manager walked up and said, "Is everything to perfection?" Every time it happens I want to scream, "No it isn't perfect." The food is good, the service is fine, but it isn't perfect.

In fact, there is nothing in this world that is perfect.

Maybe one of the reasons there is a lot of disappointment in our lives is because we've bought into the concept that something can be perfect.

Marriages are not perfect. If you want to know why your marriage isn't perfect, just take a look in the mirror. We sin, we mess up, we don't keep our word, and we fall. There will be conflict, communication problems, and setbacks. We need to be careful that we don't lead our children or others to believe that they can have perfect marriages.

Churches are not perfect. They are not perfect because they are composed of people. People just like you and people just like me. We know ourselves well enough to know that we are far from perfect, but that God loves us anyway.

Elders are not perfect. The goal of the shepherd is to follow the Chief Shepherd. His goal is to feed and guard the flock. He will make mistakes, just as we all do.

Preachers are not perfect. Those of us who preach know our own flaws and imperfections. Often times, preachers are harder on themselves than anyone else. Imperfect preachers are to point people to the Perfect Savior.

Our Lord is perfect. He never sinned. He always and only did those things that were pleasing to His Father. While we will never reach perfection in this life, we should strive with everything in us to walk in His Steps.

Dear Father, we thank You for sending Your perfect Son into the world to model for us how we should live. Please help us dear God, to walk in His steps every day of our life. We long for that day when we can see You face to face and live in Your presence for eternity. In Jesus Name we pray, Amen.

He Looked Too Much Like Jesus

Nathan Grindal had a serious problem. His problem caused him to be kicked out of a live televised dart tournament! Honestly, I had no idea that dart tournaments were that big of a deal or that they were televised.

What in the world could cause a spectator to be kicked out? He wasn't drunk, he wasn't stealing the darts, and he wasn't causing a loud ruckus. Are you ready for this?

According to the Daily Mail, Grindal "was kicked out of a live televised final after the 4,500-strong crowd interrupted play by taunting him...because he looks like Jesus."

The article goes on to state, "Chants of 'Jesus' quickly spread through the rowdy crowd packed into Butlins' at Minehead, Somerset. Security staff were called amid fears that Grindal's 'omnipresence' was upsetting the concentration of ex-world champ Taylor and his Belgian rival."

The likeness of Grindal published in the Daily Mail does in fact resemble what many believe Jesus may have looked like. The problem is, of course, that nobody knows for certain what Jesus looked like.

The real question that we need to consider is, are we as Christians ever accused of "looking like Jesus?" We are not talking here about physical appearance, but about lifestyle. Are we, as the people of God, ever accused of being like Jesus?

We know that the Word of God teaches that we are to follow in the steps of Jesus. (1 Peter 2:21) We know that we are to work to develop the mind of Christ (Philippians 2:5). We understand that we are to allow Christ to be formed in us (Galatians 4:19). We should ask ourselves regularly if this is true about our lives. When people look at our lives do they think of Jesus?

Do we look like Jesus when it comes to our commitment to the Father? Jesus explained His own commitment to the Father by saying, "I always do the things that are pleasing to Him" (John 8:29). Are we more concerned with doing what pleases us than what pleases our Father?

Do we look like Jesus when it comes to our love for others? He loved everyone so much that He was willing to die for us (John 15:13; John 3:16). Jesus' love for others could be seen in every action He performed, in every thought that entered His mind, and in every word He spoke.

Do we look like Jesus when it comes to the way we treat those who are most often overlooked? Jesus spoke to a woman that others would have nothing to do with (John 4). In fact, He traveled a great distance to be at the very spot where He encountered this woman. Most Jewish men would have traveled an even greater distance to keep from being in that place.

Do we look like Jesus when it comes to our compassion for those who are hurting? Jesus wept with close friends at the passing of their brother and His friend (John 11:35). His love for that family was evident to those who saw Him weep (John 11:36).

"Seeing the people, He felt compassion for them, because they were distressed and dispirited like sheep without a shepherd" (Matthew 9:36).

"And Jesus went forth and saw a great multitude, and was moved with compassion toward them, and he healed their sick" (Matthew 14:14).

"They said unto Him, 'Lord, that our eyes may be opened.' So, Jesus had compassion on them, and touched their eyes: and immediately their eyes received sight, and they followed him" (Matthew 20:30-34).

As we read and study the life of Jesus we will begin to look more like Him. As we glorify Him by the way we respond to our Father and by the way we treat others we will look like Him. As we seek to follow in His steps every day we will look even more like Him.

Wouldn't it be wonderful if we lived so much like Christ that when people see us they think of Jesus? It really is what people want and what they need from followers of Christ.

Dear Father, help us to look more like Jesus every day. Help us to look like Him because we always want to please You. Help us to look like Him because of our love for others. Help us, dear God, to look like Jesus because of our compassion for those who are hurting. In His name we pray, Amen.

Don't Let Them Take Away Your Faith

On our last morning in the Dominican Republic, Laura and I were sitting at breakfast with our friend Dan Coker. Brother Dan has done as much work in missions as anyone we've ever met.

He has lived an extremely interesting life. I could sit and listen to his stories forever. The last story he told us was about an experience he had several years ago to Cuba. He needed a haircut, so he went to visit a local barber. While sitting in the barber chair Dan began talking to the barber about Jesus (what a wonderful concept!).

He talked to the barber about what it means to follow Jesus, about the need to be obedient to the words of Jesus, and about giving his life completely to the

Lord. When he was leaving, the barber told Dan how much he appreciated his sharing the story of Jesus and how much it meant to him to hear the Gospel.

Then the barber told Dan that what he disliked most about the revolution in Cuba is, "They have taken away our faith!" Dan was so moved by what the barber said that he made a special trip back to take the barber some clothes and a few other items just so he could have another opportunity to talk to him about the Gospel.

That statement keeps ringing in my ear ever since Dan told us this wonderful story. "They have taken away our faith." The Bible teaches us that we gain faith through listening to the Word of God (Romans 10:17).

Many of us first heard the words of faith from our parents and grandparents. God commanded the Israelite men to teach their sons and their grandsons His commands (Deuteronomy 6:1-9).

Paul reminded Timothy of the importance of holding on to the faith that had been first in his grandmother and then in his mother (2 Timothy 1:5). If that faith is what it should be, then we will allow it to grow in us (2 Timothy 1:5).

The writer of Hebrews gives us a wonderful definition of the faith we need in our hearts. "Now faith is the assurance of things hoped for, the conviction of things not seen" (Hebrews 11:1).

The Scriptures clearly teach that a Christian can lose their faith (Hebrews 6:1-6; 2 Peter 2:20-21). Our great goal as children of God is to make sure that we don't allow anyone or anything to "take away our faith."

We should not allow our family to take away our faith. Jesus teaches us that we cannot love our family more than we love Him (Matthew 10:37-39).

We should not allow our friends to take away our faith. Anyone who has friends is blessed. However, we need to be careful that we don't value friendships more than we value the Lord.

We should not allow our careers to take away our faith. The Bible commands that we work, but we must put God above everything in our lives including work. (Matthew 6:33).

We should not allow our hobbies or recreational activities to take away our faith. The Lord wants us to enjoy life (John 10:10), but too many Christians allow their hobbies and recreational activities to crowd out their faith.

We should not allow education to take away our faith. Knowledge is good, and obtaining a good education is a worthy goal. Many wonderful Christian young people have lost that faith that was first in their parents and grandparents through secular education.

We should not allow our government to take away our faith. Paul reminded us that our citizenship (literally, our government) is in Heaven (Philippians 3:20). Some Christians seem to be more concerned about politics in their country than they are about focusing on Heaven.

We should pray for our political leaders (1 Timothy 2:2), and we should obey our political leaders as long as they do not interfere with our faith (Romans 13:1-5) .Our loyalty is always first to the Lord and His Kingdom (Matthew 6:33).

We should not allow our experiences to take away our faith. Too many times Christians go through some tragic experience or difficult time and blame it on God. May I remind you of the words of the Apostle Paul, "For this momentary light affliction is producing for us an eternal weight of glory beyond all comparison" (2 Corinthians 4:17).

We should not allow sin to take away our faith. David said, "Your Word have I treasured in my heart, that I may not sin against You" (Psalm 119:11). Even though we will be tempted, God has promised that He will always provide a way for us to overcome the temptation (1 Corinthians 10:13).

We should not allow our future to take away our faith. Thinking about and planning for the future is certainly a worthy goal. It is possible that we can become so consumed with the future that it distracts us from growing in our faith. Jesus said, "So do not worry about tomorrow; for tomorrow will care for itself. Each day has enough trouble of its own" (Matthew 6:34).

Remember, there is nothing in this life that can separate us from God's love for us (Romans 8:37-39). Therefore, every Christian should live with an attitude that says, "I will let nothing take away my faith!"

Dear Father, In a world that cries out for our attention, help us to never lose our faith. Help us to keep our focus on You. Help us, Dear Lord to love you with all that we are and all that we have. In the Name of our Savior we pray, Amen.

How Will You Preach This Sunday?

Every preacher hears the same question on a regular basis, phrased in several different ways. "What are you preaching this Sunday?" "What series are you preaching these days?" "What is your topic for the sermon this week?" I can't count the number of times I've been asked that question.

However, in more than 35 years of preaching I've never been asked the question, "How will you preach this week?" It seems to me that it is a question of vital importance to those of us who preach as well as to those who hear us.

What we preach is important and makes a difference. However, how we preach is also extremely important and makes a difference. Preachers, let's consider a few thoughts concerning how we will preach this week.

We should preach with compassion. As we study Scripture there are many times we see our Savior moved with compassion. Seeing people who were struggling with life, people who were living in sin, people who were hurting caused Jesus to have compassion for them.

"Seeing the people, He felt compassion for them, because they were distressed and dispirited like sheep without a shepherd" (Matthew 9:36). The more we come to know people, the more we will be moved by compassion. May God help those of us who preach this week to be moved with compassion.

We should preach with love. In Ephesian 4:15 Paul tells us more than just what to teach. Of course, we are to teach the Truth. But he also tells us how to teach. We must teach the Truth with a heart, a spirit, an attitude of love.

If you are struggling in your work as a preacher, if there are problems in the congregation where you work, and if you feel like you are growing weary it might help to refocus your attention to preaching the Word and loving the people to whom you preach.

We should preach with conviction. Do we really believe what we are preaching? When Peter and John were told to stop teaching about Jesus they responded by saying, "we cannot stop speaking about what we have seen and heard. Our world and the church desperately needs preachers who have been convicted like these men of God.

We need to believe that people who have not obeyed the Gospel of Jesus are lost. We need to believe that Christians who are not walking faithfully with Him are lost. Our preaching should not raise doubts about Scripture in the minds of those who hear us. Our preaching should help people become more convinced and convicted about their faith.

We should preach with passion. The Gospel message should never be boring and dry. Remember, it is Good News. We should present the Good News with excitement and passion. In Romans 1:15 Paul uses the word, "prothumon." The root word "thumos" means boiling over, hot. The idea is that Paul was on fire as he proclaimed the Good News!

Do we really mean what we are preaching? Can those who are listening tell that we mean it? Are we moved by the Gospel? Does it touch our heart? Can those who hear us understand how much we love to preach? Some of the old preachers used to tell us to either "put some fire in our sermon, or put our sermon in the fire!"

We should preach with urgency. Richard Baxter once said, "I preached as never sure to preach again and as a dying man to dying men." WOW! What urgency. We never know when we will be preaching our last sermon. As well we never know how many people who are hearing us will be listening to their last sermon.

We should all ask ourselves regularly if we are urgent about our preaching. Are we approaching our preparation and the task of proclaiming the Word as if it is the most important work in the world?

Yes, it is extremely important to ask what we will preach this Sunday, but it is also extremely important to ask how we will preach this Sunday. May we so preach and so live that we can say with Paul, I am on fire to proclaim the Good News about Jesus to everyone!

Dear Father in Heaven, please help those of us who preach this week to consider not just what we will preach, but also how we will preach. Help us, Lord, to preach with compassion, love, conviction, passion, and urgency. Help those who hear us know that we are on fire for You. In the name of Jesus, we pray, Amen!

Impressive or Impressed?

John Maxwell is a great writer who has encouraged many to become better leaders. He recently penned the following words: "Too often we think that if we can impress others, we will gain influence with them. We want to become others' heroes – to be larger than life. That creates a problem because we're real live human beings. People can see us for who we really are. If we make it our goal to impress them, we puff up our pride and end up being pretentious – and that turns people off."

Maxwell has hit the proverbial nail on the head. It seems that more people in our world are interested in being impressive than they are in being impressed. It happens all the time. It happens among adult children when there is sibling rivalry. One family member wants to outdo or one-up another family member. One family member wants to dominate the conversation and refuses to allow others to talk. One family member thinks that what they have to say is more important than what anyone else has to say.

This happens when Christians get together, and each one believes their stories are more important than all the others. It happens when one parent or grandparent only wants to talk about their family and never listens to others. It happens when one Christian is obsessed with talking about their own life (victories, joys, sorrows, etc.), yet shows little interest or concern in the lives of others.

This approach to relationships is far different from the attitude of our Lord. "Have this attitude in yourselves which was also in Christ Jesus, who, although He existed in the form of God, did not regard equality with God a thing to be grasped, but emptied Himself, taking the form of a bond-servant, and being made in the likeness of men. but emptied Himself, taking the form of a bond-servant, and being made in the likeness of men" (Philippians 2:5-8). The Apostle Paul, who penned these words, lived his life in an attempt to follow Jesus. (1 Corinthians 11:1) Notice his words that express his desire to please God rather than impress man: "But to me it is a very small thing that I may be examined by you, or by any human court..." (1 Corinthians 4:3). In Romans 12:3 he gives us this caution, "For through the grace given to me I say to everyone among you not to think more highly of himself than he ought to think."

If our goal in life is to be impressive we will mistreat others, and we will not be characterized as those who have the mind of Christ. While this attitude may be prevalent among those who do not know Jesus, it should not exist among the people of God. The world wants to impress. The child of God is interested in serving others just as our Lord served the world.

If our goal in life is to impress people with our knowledge, wisdom, and charisma, we will not be effective in winning them to the Lord. If we let those around us know how impressed we are with Jesus, we will be much more effective in leading them to the Lamb of God who takes away the sins of all men!

Dear Father, forgive us when we have tried to impress others with our life and taken the focus off of Jesus. Please help us to be impressed with His magnificence rather than trying to impress others with our own importance. In His Name we pray, Amen.

What I Want to Tell Them

Our granddaughter loves to play word games, especially with Pops! Recently while visiting our house she jumped into our bed early one morning and yelled, "Somebody's here to see you, Pops!"

She then proceeded to get me to participate in one of her word games. She wanted me to say, "One, two, buckle my shoe...Nine, ten, a big fat hen." She crawled on top of me, place her hands on my cheeks, got right in my face and said, "Pops, do you have something to say for yourself?!!"

Of course, I said exactly what she wanted me to say, and she then proceeded to the next step of the game. "Lolli, Pops said, 'nine, ten, a big fat hen.' You have to pull his ear." She loves to reproduce this game over and over and over. And of course, Lolli and Pops are more than delighted to indulge her as much as she wants.

I can't get the way she phrased the question off my mind. "Do you have something to say for yourself?" That's her way of saying, "Do you have something you need to tell me?". The answer is, I have soooo much I want to tell her! There is so much I want to say to her, her little brother, and all the other little ones who will call me "Pops."

I want to tell them how much Jesus loves them, and how much their Heavenly Father loves them.

I want to tell them to love God more than anyone or anything else.

I want to tell them how important it is to live a life that glorifies God.

I want to tell them to spend some time every day talking to their Father in Heaven.

I want to tell them to spend some time every day listening to their Father in Heaven.

I want to tell them to make sure they never forget the lessons they are learning from their parents as they grow older.

I want to tell them to remember the importance of family.

I want to tell them to be faithful to Christ and His Church all their lives.

I want to tell them that it's okay to stumble as they walk through life.

I want to tell them how important it is for them to ask for forgiveness when they fall.

I want to tell them how important it is that they learn to forgive others.

I want to tell them how important it is for them to be discerning as they listen to what teachers, preachers, leaders, etc. have to say about the Word of God.

I want to tell them to find someone to marry who will strengthen their faith in the Lord.

I want to tell them not to buy into the culture and the spirit of the age.

I want to tell them to be kind to everyone.

I want to tell them that Pops loves them more than they can know, and that he prays for them every day.

So, Evie, there is so much more, but this is part of what Pops has to say for himself. I love you, sweet girl, and your little brother, more than you'll ever know!

Dear Father in Heaven, Thank You for blessing our world and our lives with children and grandchildren. Help us to tell them the things that are most important about living for

You and glorifying You. We pray that as they grow they will want to grow in faith and in their service to You. Dear God, please protect them and guard them as they walk through life. In the name of Jesus we pray, Amen.

"My Pleasure"

In Georgia, Idaho, Alabama, Tennessee, Texas (including any of my "remote offices" around the Dallas metroplex), and in every other state, you will find a Chick-fil-a. If you express appreciation to an employee of this wonderful company, they will respond with these words: "My pleasure."

They actually seem to mean it when they say those two words. It can't just be coincidental. It must be a part of their corporate training.

It has a way of making your day better. It lifts your spirit. It has often caused me to think about how much better our world would be if Christians would use these words. After all, it is a biblical thought.

Paul expresses this sentiment well when he says, "Having so fond an affection for you, we were well pleased to impart to you not only the gospel of God but also our own lives, because you had become very dear to us" (1 Thessalonians 2:8).

The word Paul uses here is "eudokeo." It is found 21 times in the New Testament. It carries the idea of doing something willingly. The word itself suggests an attitude of joy in what we are doing.

So back to an earlier thought. What if we as God's people developed this attitude in our heart? What if we always did our work willingly? What if we always served others with joy? What if we expressed this kind sentiment to one another in all our relationships?

It is my pleasure to live a life that glorifies God. Our major purpose in this life is to give glory to God in everything we do. Whatever we do in this life should be done to His glory. (1 Corinthians 10:31) Too many times we are more concerned about our glory than about His.

It is my pleasure to treat others with kindness. We live in a world that is most often not characterized by kindness. We can make a difference in the lives of others when we have kind thoughts, when we speak kind words, and when we act in kind ways. (Ephesians 4:32)

It is my pleasure to be a servant. Our Savior taught us the meaning and the motivation for being a servant. (Philippians 2:5-8) Wouldn't it be wonderful if all of us who are servants in the church approached our work with this attitude, rather than complaining about what we do? If we want to be like Jesus, we will work to develop a servant heart!

It is my pleasure to share the message of the Gospel. When we read about our first brothers and sisters in Christ, we observe an infectious spirit as they spread the Good News everywhere they went. No wonder it was said of them, "These men who have upset the world have come here also" (Acts 17:6).

It is my pleasure to love my family. While it is certainly true that we should love everyone, it is even more important that we love those closest to us. We should have a special love for our mate (Ephesians 5:22-33), our children (Ephesians 6:1-4), and others in our family.

I encourage you to consider how much better life would be if we could say, "It is my pleasure" to perform many tasks that come our way. Wouldn't it be marvelous if we could say, "It is my pleasure" to study the Word of God, to teach Bible classes for children, to visit those who are in hospitals, to encourage the elderly and the young?

Dear Father in Heaven, as we go about our daily activities, please help us to be able to say that it is our pleasure to serve. Thank You for providing us with opportunities to show Jesus to those around us by the way we live. In the name of our Savior we pray, Amen.

Preachers...It Matters

Let's be brutally honest. There are times in our preaching and ministry that we wonder if we are doing any good. We wonder if we are accomplishing anything worthwhile for the Lord. We wonder if our work for the Lord is changing families, lives, and hearts. We wonder if what we are doing matters.

May I suggest to you as you plan to proclaim the Word of God this week, and as you minister to the lives of people you love throughout the week, that it matters, that it matters big time, that it matters eternally.

It matters to the Lord that you are involved in His work, the work of telling the world about Jesus.

It matters to the young person who needs someone else to look up to in his life.

It matters to the single mother who spends an hour or so getting her children ready for Sunday school and worship.

It matters to the young dad who desperately wants to be the spiritual leader in his home, but he needs some guidance, some help, help that you can give.

It matters to the young families whose lives are so busy and full with work, sports, school, and a million other things, but they are committed to making sure that they don't forget God.

It matters to the young single person who struggles with relationships and who continues to search for meaning, purpose, and what God wants for their life.

It matters to the teens who deep down want to do right, but they are constantly bombarded by the Evil One through drugs, alcohol, sexual temptations, and in numerous other ways.

It matters to the elderly couples who have given their lives in service to the Lord and His Church, and they want to know that what they have done/given is not in vain.

It matters to the widows and widowers who feel all alone, who long for Sunday so they can talk to someone, so they can see a smiling face, and so they can hear a kind voice.

It matters to those who refuse to allow their physical aches and pains to keep them away from the worship of the Lord.

It matters to Christians who are suffering spiritually. They know they need the Lord, and they will give it one more try.

It matters to the people who don't know the Lord yet. They are looking for something. They have a void in their heart that can only be filled by Jesus, and they need to hear a good word from the Lord.

It matters to the faithful people of God who have come to depend on you, who trust you, and who love you deeply for your commitment to the Lord.

It matters to your own family because you are providing spiritual leadership and nourishment for their lives as well as their eternity.

Don't ever let anyone tell you differently, Preacher! Don't let the devil deceive you into thinking your work is an exercise in futility. Don't let the nay-sayers bring you down. Your work, your life, and your proclamation of the unsearchable riches of Jesus matter!

Dear God, we pray that we will understand that everything we do for You, matters. Help us to do all things with the goal of glorifying You. In the Name of Jesus we pray, Amen.

You're A Real Man Now!

During a recent visit with his grandsons, one of my closest friends was showing them how he was beginning to grow a beard. His youngest grandson felt the whiskers, looked at him and said, "Paw-Paw, you're a real man now!"

Well, we all know it takes much more than a few whiskers to be a real man, right? So, what does it take? What does a real man do? How does a real man act? Allow me to make a few suggestions and please feel free to add more to the list.

Real men understand what God designed them to do.

Real men serve as spiritual leaders in their homes.

Real men regularly tell their wives they love them.

Real men listen to and value advice from their wives.

Real men put the spiritual training of their children before their jobs.

Real men lead their families in worship, and they take their families to worship.

Real men aren't afraid to say, "I was wrong," "I'm sorry," "Please forgive me."

Real men are not afraid to change the direction of their lives when they realize they are not right.

Real men are not afraid to stand up for what is right and not afraid to stand up against what is wrong.

Real men know the value of hard work, and they are not afraid to work hard.

Real men will be honest in all their dealings.

Real men build powerful friendships with other men.

Real men don't lust after women who are not their wives or who belong to another man.

Real men who are married refuse to get emotional, spiritual, or physical support from any woman other than their wives.

Real men honor their parents as long as they live.

Real men will step up and lead in the church when they are needed.

Real men are not afraid to do their best to live holy lives.

Real men listen to older men who have experienced life.

Real men invest themselves in younger men.

Real men learn from their mistakes.

Real men will be strong when they need to be and compassionate when they need to be.

Real men are not afraid to try their best to be like Jesus.

Real men spend time in the study of the Word of God.

Real men spend much time in prayer.

Real men get involved in the life of the church.

In a world with mixed up values and virtues, perhaps as much as at any time in history we desperately need some real men.

Dear God, we thank you for the strong men we have known in the past, and we pray that You will raise up more real men for our time. We pray for more men who will be leaders in their families, in our world, and in the Church. We thank you for showing us what a real man should be by sending Your Son into the world. In His strong name we pray, Amen.

"That God-Thing"

During a recent lunch with one of my favorite people, we were discussing our favorite topic. No, it wasn't the Cowboys or the Texas Rangers. We were talking about preaching. He related the following story to me.

Most mornings he stops by Whataburger for an egg and bacon bowl. Some mornings he is by himself, and some mornings he is with others. He has gotten to know some of the workers.

Recently one of the young people who works there said to him, "You are all about that God-Thing, aren't you?" She went on to tell him that she was engaged, and that her boyfriend was all about that "God-Thing." She told him that she believed in a "higher power," but not sure who or what it is. She then asked my friend if he could help her learn more.

A preacher having someone ask them to study with them about God is growing rarer these days. And, may

I add, it is a tremendous blessing and thrill when it happens!

My first thought is, "How did she know?" Did she observe my friend praying? Did she overhear him talking about the Lord? Did she observe his life?

Second, would anybody ask me that question? How about it, preacher friend, elder friend, deacon friend, Christian friend, would they ask you? Do the people who know us, or those who are strangers, ever wonder if we are all about God?

We should speak so that people will know we love the Lord (Ephesians 4:29).

We should be kind to others so that they will know we love the Lord (Ephesians 4:32).

We should talk about Jesus so that people will know we love the Lord (Acts 4:13).

We should preach so that people will know we love the Lord (2 Corinthians 4:13-18).

We should treat our brothers and sisters in such a way that people will know we love the Lord (John 13:35).

We should worship in such a way that people will know we love the Lord (1 Corinthians 14:25).

We should live so people will know that we love the

Lord (1 Timothy 4:12).

Dear Father in Heaven, please help us to be all about You and Your work. Help us to let others know about Jesus by the way we live our lives, by the way we talk, by the way we treat one another, by the way we preach. Help us, dear Lord, to be approachable so that those who do not know Jesus will want to speak with us about Him. In His precious name we pray, Amen.

Stay Focused

Jurickson Profar is just one of the young phenoms who has contributed to the success the Texas Rangers have enjoyed the last few years.

Profar was recently being interviewed by a local reporter about what he thought of some of his teammates. He was asked which teammate would most likely be a host for Saturday Night Live.

When told that it was a TV program he said he had never heard of it or watched it! He also seemed not to understand a couple of other questions he was asked that had something to do with popular culture.

Even though Profar didn't grow up in this country, he's been here long enough to know something about these topics, unless....

Unless he is so focused on learning, practicing, and playing baseball that he doesn't have time for anything else!

What if God's people were that focused? What if we were so focused on what we are about that it consumed our thinking, our time, and our lives?

I'm not saying that we should have no knowledge of the world around us. However, is it possible that we know much more about popular culture (i.e. TV shows, movies, etc.) than we do about those things that matter the most?

Where should our focus lie? Just a few thoughts for your consideration. We should…

Remain focused on giving glory to God. "…whatever you do, do all to the glory of God" (1 Corinthians 10:13).

Remain focused on spreading the Good News about Jesus. "Go therefore and make disciples of all the nations, baptizing them in the name of the Father and the Son and the Holy Spirit" (Matthew 28:18-20).

Remain focused on working to keep unity in the Body of Christ. "Being diligent to preserve the unity of the Spirit in the bond of peace" (Ephesians 4:3).

Remain focused on allowing the light of Jesus to shine through us. "Let your light shine before men in such a way that they may see your good works, and glorify your Father who is in heaven" (Matthew 5:14-16).

Remain focused on doing good to and for others. "So then, while we have opportunity, let us do good to all people..." (Galatians 6:10).

Remain focused on the study of God's Word. "Be diligent to present yourself approved to God as a workman who does not need to be ashamed, accurately handling the word of truth" (2 Timothy 2:15).

Remain focused on prayer. "Be anxious for nothing, but in everything by prayer and supplication with thanksgiving let your requests be made known to God" (Philippians 4:6).

Remain focused on Heaven and all things spiritual. "Set your mind on the things above, not on the things that are on earth" (Colossians 3:2).

In this world where there are so many distractions, we will have to work overtime to remained focused on those things that matter most.

Dear Father in Heaven, we pray that we will not become distracted by the cares and concerns of this world. Help us, Dear God to keep our eyes on You every day of our life. In Jesus Name we pray, Amen.

Is Preaching Important?

If you are not a preacher, please stop reading this now. While I am partially joking, these thoughts are written primarily with preachers in mind. Brothers, may I speak to your hearts for just a minute?

If you are like me, there may be times you wonder if the preaching you do each week is important. There are numerous reasons this could be the case. We wonder if people are listening because the building is so loud—babies are crying, people are moving around the building, cell phones are going off (argh!!), and any number of other noises are distracting.

As well, there are times it seems that the preaching is given just a passing glance in the scheduling of our worship time. There are so many announcements to be made, so many prayer requests to be mentioned, additional announcements, the man who presides over the communion time decides to preach a sermon, more announcements, an extra song, and oh, did I mention announcements???

Making sure the sermon is just the right length is one of the preacher's greatest frustrations. If it's too short, we might be accused of not being prepared or not being serious about our work. If it's too long, maybe we are monopolizing people's time, or we're accused of thinking too highly of ourselves.

PREACHING IS IMPORTANT TO GOD. Our great God is the author of the message preached (1 Peter 4:11). He is the One who chose this method of communication to save the world (1 Corinthians 1:21).

PREACHING IS IMPORTANT TO THE HEARERS. After all, one will never be able to fully come to faith without hearing the Word of God (Romans 10:17). Every week there are people who listen to the message that do not understand the importance of what they are hearing.

It is also true that some would rather have their ears tickled (2 Timothy 4:3), with commentary on the latest news, anecdotes from Dr. Phil, Oprah, or some self-proclaimed philosopher.

However, if we do our part in preaching the truth in love, proclaiming the entire counsel of God, and giving people what they truly need, the message we deliver is the most life-changing word they will ever hear.

PREACHING SHOULD BE IMPORTANT TO US. There are many areas of ministry that are extremely important. It is important when we visit someone who is in the hospital. It is important when we try to help a couple save their marriage. It is important when we attend some event of a child or young person to let them know we care about them. It is important when we assist the elders or deacons in some good work. It is important when we share the love of Christ through some kind deed.

Brothers, as important as all of this can be, there is nothing that we will do this week, or any week in our lives which is more important than proclaiming the "unfathomable riches of Christ" (Ephesians 3:8).

As we preach we must always remember that it is not about us, but it is about the power of the Gospel (Romans 1:16). May God bless you, as well as those who will hear you this week, as you preach the Word.

Dear Father, we give You thanks for Your powerful Word. May those of us who try to preach do so with all the love in our hearts. May we have love for You, Your Word, and those who listen. We pray that as we proclaim the message, lives will be forever changed. In the name of Jesus we pray, Amen.

Preachers Need Passion

"If you have a passion to do anything else, don't preach!" It's been said numerous times and in many different ways. The thought is the same, you need to want to preach more than you want to do anything else.

It has so much to do with passion!!

We need a passion for the Word of God. Paul told Timothy that preaching the Word is a very serious command (2 Timothy 4:1-3). Our number one priority as preachers is to preach the Word.

We cannot be ashamed of the Gospel (Romans 1:16). We must preach the whole purpose of God (Acts 20:27). We need preachers who have hearts that are on fire to proclaim the Word (Jeremiah 20:9; Romans 1:15). We need passion like the prophet Micaiah who said, "As the Lord lives, what my God says, that will I speak" (2 Chronicles 18:13).

We need a passion for hard work. We call it ministry. Besides telling Timothy to preach the Word, Paul also told him to, "Fulfill your ministry" (2 Timothy 4:5). That means we have much to do as we minister to others. It means we should pack it full.

One of the reasons that some preachers burn out quickly is they get bored. They don't feel like they have enough to do. We are told to put our whole heart into our work (Colossians 3:23).

The Word of God often cautions us against being lazy. A few preachers have given many preachers a bad name because of a failure to work hard.

We need a passion for people. If you can't love people you shouldn't preach. Jesus came into the world because of his love for people (John 3:16; Romans 5:8).

You can hear His passion for people in His teachings (Luke 15). You can see His passion for people in the way He was filled with compassion (Matthew 9:36; 12:7; 14:14; 15:32).

To be passionate about people will require us to spend time getting to know people. It will require us learning about their lives, their burdens, and their cares. It will require us getting involved in the lives of those to whom we preach. Some preachers spend little time among the people who hear them preach on a regular basis.

We need a passion for life. There will be times that you will feel all alone like Elijah. There will be times that you will feel that everyone is against you like Jeremiah. There will be times that even your family refuses to hear you out like Jesus.

Every person, including all preachers go through down times. Our lives are made up of peaks and valleys. We need to remember that Jesus came to bring us the abundant life (John 10:10).

The best way to survive this troubled world is to have a passion for life. As we sojourn on this earth we will enjoy it more if have a passion for life. It is also important that we show non-Christians as well as Christians how Jesus makes it possible for us to live the abundant life.

Fill your life with passion, preacher. Fill your life with passion for preaching the Word of God, passion for people, and passion for life. Your life will be a blessing and you will be blessed.

Dear Father in Heaven, please help those of us who preach Your Word to do so with passion. Help us to be passionate about Your Truth, about people, and about life. We thank you for making our lives possible. We thank You for everything You have done for us. In the Name of Jesus, we pray, Amen.

What Are You Preaching Sunday?

It's been more than two years, and I still miss those phone calls. There were long stretches of time through the years that we didn't talk that much. During the last few years of Dad's life, however, he called nearly every Saturday. It makes me wonder if he knew his time here was coming to an end.

Dad would ask about Laura and the kids. He would ask about the church. During football season, we would talk about the Alabama games. He would always ask, "What are you preaching Sunday?" It was always enjoyable to talk about the topics/themes we were preaching.

Dad would usually ask me if I had heard about a certain illustration, or if I was going to use a specific passage of scripture in the lesson. It's been two years since we've had one of those conversations, and I sure wish I could have that discussion with him again.

So, let me ask you, preacher, what are you preaching Sunday? May I make just a few suggestions? I am certain that you have your own list of thoughts as well.

This Sunday, tens of thousands of preachers will stand before churches all around the world to preach. Various topics and texts will be used to present sermons to encourage, challenge, convince, and convict those who hear them.

There is one clear mandate in scripture that should guide every man who attempts to preach. It is the mandate given by Paul to his young protégé, Timothy:

"I solemnly charge you in the presence of God and of Christ Jesus, who is to judge the living and the dead, and by His appearing and His kingdom: preach the word; be ready in season and out of season; reprove, rebuke, exhort, with great patience and instruction" (2 Timothy 4:1-2).

In this passage, we are reminded of the serious nature of our task: "I solemnly charge you..." The preaching event is not something to be taken lightly.

We are reminded of the presence of our Lord. When we preach, we stand before the God of the universe and the Savior of all men. We should be reminded that He will be with us, but also that He is listening.

We are reminded of the accountability involved. The Judge of the universe will judge both those who preach and those who listen.

We are reminded of the need to be prepared. "Be ready..." Preaching sermons that make a difference in the lives of those who listen takes a great amount of time and energy. Brothers, no one knows how much time you have put into your message other than you and the Lord. It is impossible for people who have never preached to appreciate how much is involved in preparing a sermon.

We are reminded of when we are to preach the Word of God. "...In season and out of season..." This statement simply means that we are to preach the Word of God all the time. There is never a time we should lay aside the Word of God and replace it with anything else.

We are reminded of how we are to preach the Word of God. "...Reprove, rebuke, and exhort, with great patience and instruction." There is a positive side and a negative side to how we are to preach. However, we are always to exhibit "great patience."

Preach the Word of God. The number one priority for a preacher every time he stands in front of people is to preach the Word of God. That is our mission. That is our calling. That is our charge (2 Timothy 4:1-3).

Preach the love of God. Jesus came into this world so that we would know about the love of God. He preached the love of God. Jesus died on the cross because of the love of God (John 3:16; Romans 5:8).

Preach the grace of God. Jesus came into this world to bring grace and truth (John 1:14). Some who listen to us preach believe that they are on their own. They have never learned of the amazing grace of God that saves us from our sins.

Preach the hope that Christ gives. Many of the people who will listen to you preach this weekend are hurting. Some of them are struggling in their marriages. Some of them are caught up in sin. They all need hope. It is our great privilege to offer living hope to the hungry heart (1 Peter 1:3).

Preach the peace that passes all understanding. Our world is at war. Some of those who come to worship on Sunday will be married couples who are at war. There will be parents and children who are at war with one another.

All of us are at war with Satan (Ephesians 6:10-24). How blessed we are to introduce those who hear us preach to the Prince of Peace (Isaiah 9:6).

Preach the Gospel. The Gospel is good news. The people who will sit in our buildings on Sunday will have heard hours and hours of bad news throughout the week. They are desperate for good news. We are blessed to be able to share the most valuable good news of all (Romans 1:16).

By the way, if I could talk to my dad I would tell him I'm preaching about the family. My goal is to take the Word of God and apply it to how families can be stronger as well as grow in their faith.

What are you preaching, brother? Whatever topic or text you are preaching, be certain that you are guided by the Word of God. God will be pleased, sinners will be converted, the church will be encouraged, and you will be blessed. PREACH THE WORD!

Dear Father, help those of us who endeavor to proclaim the good news to preach the truth. Help us to let people know about Your marvelous love, about Your amazing grace, about the peace that passes all understanding, and about the living hope that comes to us through Jesus. In the name of Jesus we pray, Amen.

A Special Cup of Coffee

It seems like it was about two-thirds milk and one-third coffee, with several spoons of sugar thrown in for an even richer taste! It was, with all due respect to ELF, "The World's Best Cup of Coffee!"

It happened, at most, once or twice a year. We would make the two-hour drive to visit our grandparents in north Alabama. It was always the highlight of the year for us. We loved being in their home. There was something special, something magical, about that house!

Usually it was just a day or two, maybe a week at the most, but when we were there I would get up early in the morning and sit on at the kitchen window with my maw-maw. She would make that special cup of coffee for me, and I would sit with her and watch my paw-paw leave with his employees for the work day.

She would tell me all about what the men would be doing throughout the day. I would ask questions, and she would patiently answer every question. I thought my maw-maw was the most fun person in the whole world.

Even though there were several other grandchildren in the house, I believed that she was just interested in me.

What I learned later in life was that she would have done the same for any of her grandchildren, and there were times that she spent special time with each of them.

Our Father in Heaven sent his son to die for the whole world (John 3:16; Romans 5:8). Jesus gave his life as a "ransom for all" (1 Timothy 2:6).

While it is true that God is the Savior of "all men" (1 Timothy 4:10), there is definitely a unique characteristic to the relationship He has with His followers.

As we gather for worship, may we be reminded of the fact that Jesus is the Savior of all, but the relationship we have with Him through His covenant is special indeed.

Father, help us to be mindful of the fact that You gave Your Son for everyone. Help us never forget the unique relationship we have through the covenant of His precious blood. In Jesus' name, Amen.

Five Suggestions for Working with Difficult People

Just about every preacher deals with them. You know who they are in your life. They are those cantankerous, time-consuming, whining, lazy, difficult people. It could be the church member who seems to monopolize your time because something is always wrong. Maybe it's a retired preacher who sits in your audience each week and tells you what you should have said, or what you misquoted in your sermon, or how he would have preached it.

Maybe it's a co-worker who refuses to carry his part of the load. You know, the guy who does as little as possible, just enough to get by. Or it might be an elder. The one who is always on your back, watching you like a hawk, secretly undermining and criticizing everything you do.

What's a preacher to do? What if your life and ministry is overflowing with people like this? Allow me to share a few suggestions.

Preach the Word. I'm not trying to overstate the obvious here. At times when we are dealing with difficult people we may be tempted to lash out at those who have hurt us. We may be tempted to spend an overabundance of time on some issue or struggle that we are dealing with.

This is not the time to become a "hobby-rider." It is a time to focus on our study of and our proclamation of the Word of God (2 Timothy 4:2). One reason that preaching through books of the Bible is valuable is because it keeps us focused on the Word, and we cover issues as they show up in the text.

Fulfill your ministry. Paul encouraged Timothy to fulfill his ministry (2 Timothy 4:5). This would involve staying busy in serving others. One of the very best ways to handle difficult people is by serving them, doing good deeds for them, and ministering to them.

As we remain busy in the Lord's work we will have less time to dwell on the problems caused by working with difficult people. When we are busy helping others, we have little time to be concerned about those who are difficult.

Turn problem people over to the Lord, and remember who will be your Judge and theirs. When we are dealing with difficult people, we need to spend a great deal of time in prayer for and about them. We will do our best when we turn our attitude about difficult people over to the Lord.

When we realize that there are some people that we cannot change on our own, it will be easier for us to turn them over to the Lord. Some people have been difficult for much of their lives, and they refuse to change. The best that we can do in these situations is to follow the example of Jesus (1 Peter 2:23).

Learn from criticism. If we are not careful, we will develop an attitude that says there is nothing I can learn from anybody. How can you distinguish between constructive criticism and bad criticism?

One way is to seek to consider the critic. Some people hardly ever speak to you unless it is to be critical. They are constantly criticizing. Be careful about putting stock in this critic's words. Typically, if someone writes a letter, email, etc. and refuses to sign it, the criticism isn't valid.

Some people balance constructive criticism with positive affirmation. It is wise to listen to the criticism offered by someone like this. In addition, if someone is a trusted friend who is speaking the truth in love, it would be wise to listen.

The wise man said, "Faithful are the wounds of a friend, but deceitful are the kisses of an enemy" (Proverbs 27:6).

Lean on those who encourage you. The truth is, in ministry we will all be associated with difficult people. We can't escape it. A couple of things to remember here: (1) Jesus spent time with difficult people. (2) Sometimes we might just be difficult for others!

So, learning to handle criticism is a fact of ministry. However, we don't have to spend an excessive amount of time with difficult people. It is important that we find people that we enjoy. Find people with common interests, those who are in a similar life-stage. Find people who are positive, who build you up. Surround yourself with people who will help make your ministry a joy and not a burden.

Dear Father, thank you for the many different types of people that You allow to cross the path of our lives. Help us, dear God, to be patient with and to learn how to deal with difficult people. Help us to learn to follow in the steps of Jesus. In His precious name we pray, Amen.

Remember

U.S. Navy Veteran Ron White memorized nearly 7,000 words and more than 2,200 names. Let that sink in for just a moment. To put it in perspective, that would be like memorizing Psalm 119!

The U.S. veteran recorded the names of the military fallen in Afghanistan on a makeshift wall in downtown Fort Worth...and he did it all from memory. He said, "I have pictures in my mind for each name." It took White, who served in Afghanistan in 2007, about ten months to memorize all those names.

Although he made the news and many people came to watch what he did, White said he wasn't doing it for the attention. "I would have done this in a field by myself if no one showed up, just because it's something I wanted to do."

To remember those who gave their lives for our country in this way is a very honorable deed. There are numerous ways that we remember those who have served us and have sacrificed for us and the lives of those we love.

God has blessed us with the marvelous gift of memory and His Word has much to say about remembering.

"Remember the word that I said to you, 'A slave is not greater than his master.' If they persecuted Me, they will also persecute you; if they kept My word, they will keep yours also" (John 15:20).

"Remember that you were at that time separate from Christ, excluded from the commonwealth of Israel, and strangers to the covenants of promise, having no hope and without God in the world" (Ephesians 5:12).

"I thank God, whom I serve with a clear conscience the way my forefathers did, as I constantly remember you in my prayers night and day" (2 Timothy 1:3).

"But remember the former days, when, after being enlightened, you endured a great conflict of sufferings" (Hebrews 10:32).

"Remember the prisoners as though in prison with them, and those who are ill-treated, since you yourselves also are in the body" (Hebrews 13:3).

"Remember those who led you, who spoke the word of God to you; and considering the result of their conduct, imitate their faith" (Hebrews 13:7).

"That you should remember the words spoken beforehand by the holy prophets and the commandments of the Lord and Savior spoken by your apostles" (2 Peter 3:2).

"But you, beloved, ought to remember the words that were spoken beforehand by the apostles of our Lord Jesus Christ" (Jude 1:17).

"'Therefore remember from where you have fallen, and repent and do the deeds you did at first; or else I am coming to you and will remove your lamp stand out of its place— unless you repent" (Revelation 2:5).

"So remember what you have received and heard; and keep it, and repent. Therefore, if you do not wake up, I will come like a thief, and you will not know at what hour I will come to you" (Revelation 3:3).

Is there someone you should remember and give thanks for today? How long has it been since you have said thank you to someone you need to remember? Do you remember those who have sacrificed for you through a life of thanksgiving?

Maybe it's our parents who gave us life, sacrificed so that we could enjoy life, or taught us the Word of God.

Maybe it's the person who led you to Christ through the Word of God.

Maybe it's your mate who has stood by you through the storms and trials of life.

Maybe it's a friend who has been beside you through some particularly difficult time.

May I encourage you to take the time to remember someone who has been special to you? Take the time to express your gratitude to them. Take the time to show them your appreciation by the way you live your life. Take the time to thank God for all He has done. Remember.

Dear Father, thank You for the gift of memory. Thank You for those who have sacrificed to make our lives better. Thank You, dear God, for the people who helped us learn about You. Help us to remember and to be thankful. In the name of Jesus we pray, Amen.

A Birthday Thought

Please indulge me for just a few thoughts. Today would have been Dad's 77th birthday. There has not been one day since his passing that we have not thought about him. So many times we have wanted to pick up the phone to call him.

We would just love to hear his voice, to get a bit of advice, to ask him what he thought about a church issue, to talk about sermons, to ask him about a family issue, and a million other things. Dad was always a man of few words, but when he spoke it was always meaningful, thoughtful, and helpful.

Rather than a lot of talk, Dad was a man of action who was always serving others. He cared about others more than he cared about himself. More than anything else, he was concerned about the souls of men. He wanted everyone he knew to learn about the saving message of the Gospel. He wanted people who had fallen away from the Lord and His church to come home.

He was more focused on Jesus than anyone we have ever known. He preached about Jesus, and he allowed Jesus to shine through him. He was always doing for others. He did for others without people knowing about it.

He was unassuming in his service to others. He didn't serve to be seen or known of men. He served because he was trying to follow in the steps of Jesus. He served because he had the heart of a servant. He served because he genuinely cared about people. He served because it allowed him the opportunity to reach people with the Gospel.

Dad was a humble man. As we get older, the more it becomes clear just how much humility he had in his life. We also understand how much humility filled his heart when we see so many preachers who are all about themselves. They promote themselves. They always talk about themselves in their sermons, in their writings, and in their conversations with others.

Unfortunately, humility is rare in the lives of many Christians, and it seems especially true in preachers. It is difficult to understand because, of all people, Christians should understand the need for humility. Even more so, preachers, who regularly study the life of Jesus and who tell others about Him, should develop more humility.

To my preaching brothers, we need to pray more that God will help us not focus our work and our lives on ourselves. We need to work harder to reach out to others, to help others, and to live for others. We need to promote ourselves less and promote the Lord more. In a world where people all around us are hurting, they need less of us and more of Jesus.

Dad would often quote the following words from an old hymn. "For others, Lord, for others, let this my motto be. Help me to live for others, that I might live like Thee." He believed those words, and he lived them more than anyone I have ever known.

While Dad was a humble man, he was not weak. His faith was strong, his preaching was strong, and his commitment to the Lord was strong. He would not allow others to run roughshod over the Lord, the truth, or the church. He always defended the faith in a spirit of love.

He defended those who could not defend themselves. He looked out for and cared for people that had no one to care for them. He built friendships for the Lord based on the individual's need for Jesus rather than what they could do for him.

Dad was more interested in promoting Jesus and His church than he was in promoting himself. As far as we know, Dad never asked someone to schedule him to preach in a meeting or a conference. He would accept those invitations, but he did not promote himself.

Unlike some preachers we have known, he would never tell a church how much they should pay him. He didn't have a fee for speaking. He would at times preach for no remuneration. We heard about a preacher who one time gave the check back to the church and told them he was embarrassed by the amount. Something like that would have been unthinkable to Dad. He was not into playing church politics or games that so many want to play in the church. He was about preaching the Word of God and doing the work of God.

Dad would not care much for the words written here. He would say it was too much about him. But these are the thoughts that I wanted to share with others today, especially other preachers. Even in Dad's writing and teaching, if he was saying something about himself he wouldn't use the word, "I." He would say "we" but not "I." Some would argue that we should use "I" because it personalizes or humanizes our thoughts. Dad would say we don't need to personalize or humanize, we need to present Jesus. These thoughts are written not because they are about my dad, but because they are about our Father in Heaven and our Savior. It is not my intention to be unkind to others, but it is my intention to encourage all of us who claim to represent Christ to do better at presenting Christ rather than ourselves.

There are so many characteristics that Dad displayed every day that we long to develop in my own lives. Not just because we want to be more like my dad, but because we are convinced that he wanted to be like Jesus. We understand fully that he was not the only person in the world who was like this. There are many of you who are reading this who could say similar things about your parents. If that is true, praise God for your loved ones. If we have been blessed with parents like this, we should do our best to follow the path they carved out for us.

Dad always had a smile on his face and a song in his heart. He believed in hope, he had a positive attitude about life, and he believed that God would take care of those who trusted in Him. He believed that there was good in every human being. He believed that God has placed eternity in the heart of every person, and because of that, every person deserves the opportunity to hear the Gospel.

My sincere prayer is that all of us who endeavor to preach the Gospel will be more like this. That we will all allow the glory of God to be seen in us. That we will let our lights shine before men so that they might glorify God. "For God, who said, 'Let light shine out of darkness,' has shone in our hearts to give the light of the knowledge of the glory of God in the face of Jesus Christ" (2 Corinthians 4:6).

Dear Father in Heaven, we thank You for bringing people into our lives who show us the way to You. We thank You for people who allow Jesus to be seen in them. Help us all, dear God, to be more like Jesus. Help us to share the message of Jesus and the love of Jesus with everyone we can. Help us, Lord, to make our lives about You and not about us. In His precious name we pray, Amen.

Our God Can, Our God Will

A couple of years ago, while attending a Texas Rangers game with some close friends, I saw something that I'll never forget. We watched a fan reach for a foul ball over a railing, and he fell thirty feet from the upper deck to the ground level bleachers.

Thankfully, the gentleman survived the fall, but seeing what happened left me with an eerie, empty, helpless feeling. I so wanted to reach out across the stadium and help the man, but I was powerless to do so.

My desire to help could not overcome my inability to help. It seems like that is the way it is with many situations. We want to help people who are falling. We want to help families that are struggling. We want to help fellow Christians who are going through difficult times. But, more often than not, we are unable.

Imagine another scenario. Imagine someone sitting close to that falling fan that could have reached out to save him, but refused to so do so because of a lack of concern or some other reason.

As it concerns our salvation there is only one who has both the ability and the willingness to save us. How blessed we are to serve a God who can save us and who will save us.

> "And you were dead in your trespasses and sins, in which you formerly walked according to the course of this world, according to the prince of the power of the air, of the spirit that is now working in the sons of disobedience... But God, being rich in mercy, because of His great love with which he loved us, even when we were dead in our transgressions, made us alive together with Christ (by grace you have been saved), and raised us up with Him, and seated us with Him in the heavenly places in Christ Jesus, so that in the ages to come He might show the surpassing riches of His grace in kindness toward us in Christ Jesus" (Ephesians 2:1-7).

Our God is rich in mercy and in love. He has the power to make us alive together with Christ. He made this possible by allowing Jesus to die for us (Romans 5:8). God has both the power to save and the desire to save. Praise God. God can, and God will.

As we gather this Sunday to observe the memorial feast, let us be thankful that our God can and our God will save us from falling!

Dear Father, we are thankful that You have both the power and the willingness to reach out to save us when we are falling. Help us, dear God, to remember as we gather around the table that Christ sacrificed his life so that we may live. In His name we pray, Amen.

Are You Growing in Your Faith?

Some of the greatest blessings of my life are the men that God has brought into my life. I am thankful for the men who are a part of my family. My son, my son-in-law, my grandson, my brother, and an adopted son all mean more to me than life itself.

The veteran preachers who have mentored me have been a profound blessing to my life. My life has also been richly blessed because I have the opportunity to mentor some younger men. The preachers who are my closest friends, by virtue of age and life stage, are a part of my life's greatest blessings.

There are also many men in the church, as well as some out of the church, who are a tremendous blessing to my life.

There are four men who are especially a rich blessing to my life. None of them are preachers. We have traveled together, shared many, many meals together, laughed together, cried together, and prayed together. These friends would do anything in the world for me, and I would do anything that I possibly could for any one of them.

One of the things I love most about these guys is to hear them pray. They don't pray like most of the preachers I've listened to in my life. Not that there is anything at all wrong with the way preachers pray.

My friend's prayers are from deep in their hearts, they are extremely honest, and they challenge me to be a better man. One of my friends says at some point in every prayer I've heard him pray, "Help us to grow in our faith."

What a tremendous request that we should all consider on a regular basis. "Help us grow in our faith." Are we growing in our faith? Do we really want to grow in our faith? How can we experience growth in our faith?

We grow in our faith through the study of the Word. Whenever we study the Word of God we increase our faith, and we grow. That is what He wants for all His children (1 Peter 2:2; 2 Peter 3:18; Hebrews 5:12-14; 1 Timothy 4:13).

We grow in our faith through prayer. Prayer has been called our lifeline to God. It is our way of communicating to Him the desires of our hearts. Just as a husband and wife need to communicate with one another to strengthen their marriage, we should communicate with God to strengthen our relationship with Him (1 Thessalonians 5:17; Philippians 4:6; Hebrews 4:14-16).

We grow in our faith through worship. The more time we spend worshipping our Lord, the more we will grow in our faith. We should work hard to find times for private worship and family worship. We should do everything possible to worship with the Body of Christ whenever worship takes place (Hebrews 10:23-25).

We grow in our faith through fellowship. The more time we spend with others who are trying to grow in their faith, the more we will grow in ours. We should find people who have common goals, interests, and dreams. We should associate with people who will build us up rather than those who will drag us down (1 Corinthians 15:33; 1 Timothy 4:12).

We grow in our faith through the trials of life. No one enjoys facing trials and difficulties in this life. No one looks forward to them. Yet the Scriptures teach us that as we endure the trials of life properly we will grow in our faith (James 1:2-4; 1 Peter 1:6-9). Even our Savior grew as He suffered in this life (Hebrews 5:8).

These are just a few of many ways that will help us grow in our faith. My prayer for you is that every day and in every circumstance of your life you will grow in your faith. With God's help and our commitment to Him we can all be stronger in our faith with every passing year.

Dear Father in Heaven, we want to grow in our faith. We want to be more like Jesus every day. We want to bring glory to You and Your Son in everything we do. Help us, dear God, to work diligently every day to grow in our faith. In the name of our Savior we pray, Amen.

Do You Want to Keep Your Preacher?

As I begin to write these thoughts, I must do so with a disclaimer. I have been a full-time preaching minister for 32 years. I have been preaching now for nearly 40 years. I have been a part of a preaching family all my life. My family has always been well taken care of during these years.

I am not writing these words because of anything I need, or as a hint to my current congregation. Allow me to be blunt. The fact is, if I could write this without my elders or the members of the Lewisville church reading it I would. You folks who are a part of the Lewisville church are some of the kindest and most generous people on the face of the earth.

I am writing this because I know too many preachers who have not been blessed in the numerous ways that my family has been blessed. I am writing to encourage elders and churches to rethink how they show appreciation to their ministers.

Some of the thoughts I will sharing here have happened to me personally. I do not publish them to boast, but with the sincere hope that some churches and Christians will find creative ways to express appreciation to the men who serve as their ministers.

I believe that many churches love their preachers but have never been taught how to show that love to them. My sincere prayer is that these words will be helpful and that it will be received in the spirit in which was written.

Oh, and one more disclaimer. This only applies if you really want to keep your preacher. If you don't want to keep him there is no need for you to pay attention any further.

Tell him you appreciate his preaching. You can tell him face to face. You can send him a note. I have in my files notes of encouragement that have come from church leaders and church members through the years. They are some of my most prized possessions. These days you can send emails, text messages, Facebook messages, etc. There are many great ways to say, "I am thankful for you."

Tell him you appreciate his work. When a minister does something special for your family, let him know how much you appreciate it. Most ministers will serve whether they receive appreciation for it or not. However, it will strengthen your minister greatly if he knows you appreciate it when he has done something special for you or your family.

Show your preacher's family you appreciate them. Do your best to provide for the needs of the preacher's family. Try to refrain from making the preacher's family live in a glass house. Give the preacher's family the opportunity to fit in and be a part of the congregation.

Let your preacher know you are praying for him. Most church members I know pray regularly for their ministers as well as their minister's family. It will be a great source of strength if you tell him/them personally that prayers are being offered.

Show your preacher you appreciate him. This is not about money or things. It is about showing appreciation. It is about recognizing the ministers who are doing a good job.

One church I know about gives each of their ministers an end of the year bonus. It is based upon years of service and there are incremental increases the longer a minister works with the church.

Another church I know about called the four ministers in at the end of the year. They presented each of them with a new iPad and told them that they would receive a five percent increase in their salary. Now that's concrete evidence that says, "We are thankful for you and we want you to stay with us for a long time."

Other churches have given their preachers an extra week of vacation, a sabbatical, or some additional time off just to spend relaxing with his family. One church I know about sent their preacher and his wife on a cruise. Another church years ago gave their preacher a new car.

There are numerous ways you can show appreciation to your minister. Buy him a book, or pay for some of his gas for all the visits and calls he makes. Take him and his family out for a meal or just hand them a gift card for their favorite restaurant.

As long as I live, I'll never forget the family who bought me a suit one time because I had ministered to their family. It was a suit that I could have never purchased for myself.

When I was a very young preacher, a family called me to their home and said we want you to know how much we appreciate what you have done for us. We would like to pay for you to go to the Holy Lands. That trip changed by life and made me a better preacher. I will forever be thankful for this wonderful family.

I'm not saying that every church can or even should follow these exact suggestions. I'm just encouraging you to do something to let your ministers know you appreciate them.

Some churches take the approach that we pay our ministers well, so we don't need to give them bonuses, raises, and gifts of appreciation. I would argue that you should, if you want them to feel appreciated and wanted.

Another benefit of showing appreciation to your ministers is they will work even harder. Even the most self-motivated people will be motivated more when they feel wanted and appreciated.

The elders or leaders of the church are the only ones who can carry out some of these suggestions. However, the suggestions about words and notes of appreciation are something that anyone can do.

Most preachers I know would never express these kinds of thoughts to their elders or the church for fear that they will be looked upon as seeking the wrong kind of praise as well as being considered money-hungry. Most preachers I know would do what they do even if they never received any appreciation.

While it may be that there are a few who do seek the wrong kind of praise and are money-hungry, my conviction is that this is not true of the large majority of preachers.

Preachers are human. They have frailties in their lives. They need encouragement, and they need to be appreciated like every other person in the world. And just in case anyone thinks we are being too easy on preachers, just wait for the article to preachers about "Do You Want to Keep Your Job?!!"

I hope that church leaders, as well as all church members who read this, will make the effort to let your preacher know how much you appreciate him. And I hope you will do it soon.

Holy Father, we thank you for the opportunity to be a part of Your Church. We are thankful for every person who is a part of the Body of Christ. Help us, dear God, to show one another how much we appreciate each other. Help us to allow the light and the love of Jesus to be seen through us. In His wonderful name we pray, Amen.

Wisdom from 7-Eleven

On my way to the hospital early one morning I stopped off at a 7-Eleven to get me a French Vanilla Cappuccino.

I know this is going to be heresy to some, but I like their Cappuccino better than Starbucks. There, I said it, sorry to those who are offended. And dare I mention the price difference!

Not that I have anything against Starbucks. In fact, I enjoy going from time to time to get some serious reading and studying done. You can't always find a good spot at my regular office (for those of you don't know me well, that would be Chick-fil-A).

Well, on this particular morning I got more than a cup of coffee. I received some great life wisdom from the guy behind the counter at 7-Eleven.

He and his co-worker were having a conversation. She was decrying the fact that another co-worker had not done his job correctly the night before. She had to complete his work, and she was letting him have it.

Then it came. The guy behind the counter said, "It's just like relationships, there's always room for improvement." Not sure if he knew it or not, but he spoke volumes with that statement.

Now that's a morsel of wisdom that all of us could use. How often are we guilty of expecting perfection from the people closest to us? Have we forgotten that there are no perfect people?

Do we expect perfection from our mate, our children, our parents, and other family members? Do we expect perfection from our elders, preachers, youth ministers, and other workers in the Church? Do we expect perfection from our employees or employers?

When we demand or expect perfection, we will be sorely disappointed. I can think of at least two reasons this is true.

Perfection is not possible. The truth is we all sin (Romans 3:9-10,23; 1 John 1:8), and we can never reach perfection in this life.

Perfection is not practical. If everyone were perfect (like some think they are), we could not know the joy of forgiving and extending grace to others.

Next time you start demanding perfection from someone close to you remember this morsel of wisdom from the guy at 7-Eleven. There's always room for improvement (even in your life)!

Dear God, we pray that we will never get to the point in our life where we believe we have arrived. We pray that we will never quit growing and that we will never quit working to become more like Jesus. In His Wonderful Name we pray, Amen.

My Father's Writing

It is difficult to believe that it has been two years since Dad passed away. During the past two years, I have thought about my Dad every single day. Some days are more difficult than others.

So many times I wish I could call Dad just to hear his voice, to listen to his wisdom. So many times I would like to ask his advice about a sermon, a problem at church, or a family situation.

One of the things I have always loved about Dad was his ability to put his thoughts into print. I love his writings. One of my most prized possessions is Dad's copy of his master's thesis from Harding Graduate School. It is titled, "Pisteuo in the Fourth Gospel." It is an outstanding treatment of faith in the book of John. I read it again recently and loved every word of it.

Another one of my most prized possessions is a collection of Bibles that belonged to Dad. There was a time when Dad did most of his preaching from small New Testaments. I have the last two that he used in his preaching. They are full of notes. On some pages there are so many notes it is difficult to read them all. His thoughts as he studied the Word of God amaze me. I thank God that we had a father who taught us to love God's Word.

Some of my favorite memories include being able to be at 34 Freed Hardeman Lectureships with Dad. It was one of the highlights of my life to sit with Dad through hundreds of lectures. He always had a small writing pad with him, and he took notes on every lecture he heard.

Through the years as we would sit in Lloyd Auditorium or Old Chapel Hall I would watch what Dad wrote. Many times I have copied in my notes what he wrote. In Dad's later years he would occasionally doze off during a lecture. I now believe it was because he was wearing himself out.

Dale and I would sometimes laugh because you could tell when Dad would doze off as his handwriting would trail off. His handwriting was also affected in his later years because Dad had a form of Parkinson's disease.

I loved Dad's writing because it was always true to the Word of God, it was always insightful, it was always kind, and it was always helpful. And as much as I love

Dad's writing, I love my Father in Heaven's writing even more.

Our Father's writing provides everything we need in this life for godly living (2 Peter 1:3).

Our Father's writing helps us stay away from sin (Psalm 119).

Our Father's writing helps us maintain a balanced life (Joshua 1:6-9).

Our Father's writing illuminates our way (Psalm 119:111).

Our Father's writing tells us about Jesus (John 21:20-21).

Our Father's writing tells us how much He loves us (John 3:16).

Our Father's writing reveals to us His heart.

Our Father's writing shows us the way to Heaven.

Our Father's writing tells us how we can find contentment in this life.

Our Father's writing teaches us how to treat others.

Our Father's writing helps us reflect on who we really are.

Our Father's writing instructs us, corrects us, and is very profitable (2 Timothy 3:16).

I hope we don't ever forget the value in our Father's writing, and we take time to soak in what He has written every day of our lives.

Dear God, thank You for revealing Yourself to us through Your Word. May we spend time every day of our life with Your writings. In Jesus Name we pray, Amen.

We've Got to Do This Quickly

For those of you who know me well the next sentence you read will be shocking. I replaced our hot water heater (in our attic)!! Before you have a coronary, let me set your mind at ease.

I sort of replaced our hot water heater. It had been making terrible noises (how is that for being technical?) for months. We found a replacement at Lowe's in the clearance section. It had several dents. I got the manager to come off the clearance price (just because I can't buy anything without asking if they will sell it cheaper. It's a disease!).

I called one of my best friends, and he said he would help me. Okay, he said he would do it, and I could help him. We decided to do it ourselves without getting additional manpower (bad, bad idea).

My friend has an electric wench that would be perfect for getting the new heater into the attic. We tied a rope around the hot water heater. Then we drilled a couple of holes in the attic. He stood up in the attic operating the wench, and I stood below guiding the water heater (another bad idea). We almost cleared the attic ladder when the rope slipped, and the water heater starting coming down toward me.

The wench was still holding and the ladder was helping, but most of the weight was coming down on me. My friend was trying to figure out what we should do next. I was growing more concerned. I yelled up to him, "We've got to do this quickly!"

Fortunately, we were able to lift it up into the attic and get it installed. There was a brief period of time where I thought it was going to come crashing down on me. Looking back on it, it was a blast. I think I would do it again!

My friend got a big laugh out of my "We've got to do this quickly!" statement. Since then I've been thinking about how there are so many things in life that need to be done quickly but take a massive amount of time.

It is true that nothing worthwhile is simple. Everything important that needs to be done takes a lot of time and effort. However, there are some things that need to be done quickly. At least we need to get started quickly.

Fathers who are not spending time with their families need to get started quickly.

Men who don't tell their wives they love them need to change quickly.

Women who don't respect the spiritual leadership of their husbands need to start quickly.

Married couples that don't communicate need to get started quickly.

Married couples that need to see a counselor should get started quickly.

If there is someone you need to thank, please do it quickly.

If there is someone you need to contact to express your love, please do it quickly.

Make up your mind that nothing is going to keep you from going to Heaven, and do it quickly.

If there is someone you need to talk to about Jesus, go do it quickly.

If there is someone you need to pray for, do it quickly.

If there is something you need to do for the Lord, please get started quickly.

If there are bad habits in your life, you need to change them quickly.

If you need to repent of some sin, please do it quickly.

If there is something you need to do for someone else, do it quickly.

If you need to start studying your Bible more, do it quickly.

If you need to start praying more, by all means, do it quickly.

Dear God, we pray that we will be able to live with urgency. We pray that we will remember that our time on earth is brief. Help us, Father, to spend too much time with the trivial matters of this life. In the Name of Jesus we pray, Amen.

"I Will Never Be Lost!"

We recently hosted our annual "Sending Them Off with Prayer" night at the Lewisville church. It has become one of our favorite events each year.

We pray for everyone involved in the beginning of a new school year. If you are not doing something like this in your home church, please allow me to encourage you to do so. If you have questions about how it is done, please feel free to contact me.

This year we added something new. We gave Bibles to all our children who are entering the first grade. We called them to the front of the auditorium with their parents, and I presented them with a Bible. They were all excited, and it was a great night for all of us.

One of our parents sent me a picture of her little girl in bed the night before her first day of school, and she is holding her Bible.

Another one of our students came up to me during the next church service and said, "Mr. Jeff, look, I brought my new Bible!"

Another parent sent me the following story about her daughter.

"Avery was SO EXCITED tonight when she received her Bible at church. She quickly noticed it had a map in the back. She looked up at me and said, 'Mommy look, it has a map, now I will never be lost.' I smiled and thought to myself, you are right…this Bible is your map so you will never be 'lost.'"

How precious is that? What's that old saying, "out of the mouth of babes?" Not sure if this precious little girl realizes it or not, but she has spoken a deep theological truth!

THE BIBLE IS OUR ROADMAP TO HEAVEN. As we navigate the path of life, the Bible guides us through the rough places, the dark places, the hills, and the valleys (Psalm 119:105).

THE BIBLE IS THE ONLY BOOK THAT WILL KEEP US FROM BEING LOST. I'm certainly not opposed to reading. In fact, I love reading. It is one of my favorite pastimes. We can gain insight, encouragement, and strength from reading good books, but there is no book, other than the Word of God, that will lead us to Heaven.

THE BIBLE IS THE ONLY BOOK THAT CAN KEEP US FROM SIN. David said, "Your word I have treasured in my heart, that I may not sin against You" (Psalm 119:11). The Word of God contains the answer to sin, the remedy for sin, and the freedom from sin that we all desperately need.

THE BIBLE ANSWERS LIFE'S TOUGHEST QUESTIONS. The answers offered in the Bible are time-tested. They have been proven to work over and over again. In God's Word, we read about real people who faced the same issues that we face in our lives.

THE BIBLE PROVIDES COMFORT & STRENGTH FOR DIFFICULT DAYS. One of the greatest blessings of the Word of God is the fact that we can find comfort during tough times. "Therefore let us draw near with confidence to the throne of grace, so that we may receive mercy and find grace to help in time of need" (Hebrews 4:16). The God of all comfort (2 Corinthians 1:3-5) has a door that is always open to offer us comfort, strength, and hope.

Many seek answers to life's questions from other sources. Many turn away from the Word of God and depend on the ideas, thoughts, and words of others.

Thank you, Avery, for reminding all of us that as long as we have the Bible we will never be lost.

Dear Father, we give You thanks for your marvelous Word. Help us to remember that as long as we have the Bible we will never be lost. Help us, dear God, to cling to Your Word, to follow Your Word, to gain strength from Your Word, and most of all to obey Your Word. In the name of Jesus we pray, Amen.

"Why Am I Here?"

It was a brief acceptance speech, but it was one of the most moving, heartfelt speeches I've ever heard. A friend sent it to me. I didn't hear it live, or see it live, but I will see it and hear it again.

Gerda Weissmann Klein, a Holocaust survivor and subject of the Best Documentary Short Subject, "One Survivor Remembers," spoke deeply about her freedom. Unlike others, she did not push any social agenda, and her speech was not an exercise in self-aggrandizement. The question that Klein raises in the following comments is one that every Christian should ask.

> "...I have been in a place for six incredible years where winning meant a crust of bread and to live another day. Since the blessed day of my liberation I have asked the question, 'Why am I here...?'"

Why am I here?

Some are here to make a fortune.

Some are here to become famous.

Some are here to become president or CEO of a company.

Some are here to show others their abilities.

Some are here to create havoc, unrest, and confusion in our world.

Some are here to show the love of God to others.

Some are here to be leaders in the church.

Some are here to make the world a better place to live.

Some are here to share the burdens that others carry.

Some are here to show children the way.

Some are here to strengthen young people and families in the church.

Some are here to give to others.

Some are here to encourage those who are hurting.

Some are here to comfort the brokenhearted.

Some are here to let the light of Jesus shine in this dark world.

Some are here to lift up the hurting in prayer.

Some are here to help feed the hungry.

Some are here to help heal the sick.

Some are here to discover, invent, and create.

Some are here to love those who are broken.

Some are here to equip the saints.

Some are here to preach the Word to the church and the lost.

Some are here to teach those who do not know Jesus.

Some are here to show the way.

Some are here to glorify God.

Some are here to help us learn how to endure suffering as a Christian.

Some are here to show what it means to be a servant.

Some are here to remind us of what it means to live for Jesus.

Some are here to teach us how to die.

Some are here to teach us how to live.

Some are here to teach us how to love.

Why are you here?

Dear Father, help us to find our place in this world. Help us, dear Lord, to make sure that we understand Your purpose for our lives. Thank You for sending Jesus to show us the way. In His wonderful name we pray, Amen.

Is This the Place?

It seems that everywhere we went in the Bible lands the question was asked.

Is this the place?

Is this really the place where Jesus...?

Some of the sites are authentic. For instance, there is no question about the Sea of Galilee. You can take a boat ride on the Sea of Galilee, and you can know that our Lord was in that place. It is a very moving experience.

Some of the sites are guesses. One of my personal favorites in Israel is Gordon's Calvary and the Garden Tomb. We can't know for sure if this is the place where Jesus was crucified and buried.

Even still, one of the most thrilling experiences in my life is to stand in that tomb and sing, "Up from the Grave He Arose!"

But, back to our question, "Is this the place?" It's a question that needs to be asked about the Church. Preachers, worship leaders, elders, and everyone involved should consider this question.

"IS THIS THE PLACE?"

IS THIS THE PLACE where Jesus is exalted (Revelation 4-5)?

IS THIS THE PLACE where God is glorified (Ephesians 3:21)?

IS THIS THE PLACE where the Word of God is preached (2 Timothy 4:1-3)?

IS THIS THE PLACE where the lost can find Jesus? (1 Corinthians 14:24-25)?

IS THIS THE PLACE where we bear one another's burdens (Galatians 6:1-2)?

IS THIS THE PLACE where we saints are edified (Hebrews 10:23-24)?

IS THIS THE PLACE where we come to cast our cares on Him (1 Peter 5:7)?

IS THIS THE PLACE where we can freely confess our sins to one another (James 5:16)?

IS THIS THE PLACE where there is no favoritism (James 2:2-9)?

IS THIS THE PLACE where children are loved and taught how to love others (Matthew 18:2-5)?

IS THIS THE PLACE where the aging are given the care and concern they need (Acts 6)?

IS THIS THE PLACE where the "one another" scriptures are practiced?

IS THIS THE PLACE where God's Grace is dispensed in large doses to those who need it most?

IS THIS THE PLACE where forgiveness can be sought and offered?

IS THIS THE PLACE where anyone can come to experience the abundant life (John 10:10)?

Every one of us who is a part of the church needs to ask ourselves often, "IS THIS THE PLACE?"

Dear Father, help us all of us who are in the church to do our part to make sure that this is the place. Help us to make this place a place of joy, happiness, contentment, and peace. In the name of the One who gave us "the place" we pray, Amen.

Redeeming Value???

As those of you who are members at Lewisville know, we are working our way through the book of Genesis on Sunday nights this year. Well, sort of. We are nearly half way through the year, and we just completed Genesis chapter 4.

At our current rate, our study of Genesis will take another year or so to complete. We are committed to studying the entire book; therefore, we will take whatever amount of time is needed.

I don't know how folks who are listening to the lessons feel about the study, but I know I am loving it. I've never studied Genesis as much as I am right now. There is so much rich material in this book of beginnings.

There is so much here that helps us learn more about our great God and how He wants us to live our lives.

There is so much about how we should relate to Him as well as how we should relate to one another.

In Genesis chapter 4, we spent several weeks investigating the family of Cain and the family of Seth. We learned that the line of Cain was a remarkable family. His descendants were inventors, they were builders of cities, and they created an entire society.

The descendants of Cain perfected farming, they invented metallurgy, they invented music, and so much more.

By the way, our first ancestors were not "cavemen" as they are often portrayed in literature and the news. They were geniuses. After all, they lived hundreds of years and had plenty of time to perfect their craft.

But there is something that is clearly missing in the family of Cain. There is no mention of God. They built a society that forgot about God.

On the other hand, we learn that in the line of Seth, at least some of them attempted to turn men back to God. Then men began to call upon the name of the Lord (Genesis 4:26). Do you think it is coincidental that our Savior came through the line of Seth (Luke 3)?

So, what does all of this mean to those of us who are living in America today?

It should cause us to consider deeply the question, "What kind of society are we building?"

Obviously, there are some in our country who are great society builders. They are geniuses when it comes to technology, science, education, the arts, etc. The question is, in this rush to create, invent, and perfect, are we forgetting about God?

All the technology, education, and knowledge in the world, apart from Jesus Christ, will not save us. There is no redeeming value in our inventions, creations, and education.

During our weekly prayer breakfasts, if we discussed technology, our dear friend, Doug Lawyer, would remind us, "Boys, remember, there are no souls in those computers."

I know that some of you may be thinking, "HE WAS WRONG." It is true that these wonderful tools can be used to reach people in ways that nothing else can. And I believe that we should use them.

We can use these tools to reach out to old friends. We can use them to make new friends for the Gospel. We can use them to advertise special events. Some people will not communicate in any other way; therefore, we should communicate with them through email, texting, Facebook, etc.

Yet in and of themselves, like the inventions of the family of Cain, they have no redeeming value. So, what does have redeeming value?

RELATIONSHIPS. First and foremost is our relationship with our Lord. It is through Jesus Christ that we find salvation (John 14:6). It is through Jesus that we find peace (Matthew 11: 28-29). It is through Jesus that we find hope (1 Peter 1:3). It is through Jesus that we can talk with our Father (1 Timothy 2:5).

In addition, our relationships with fellow Christians are so vitally important to our walk with the Lord. (Philippians 3:15-17). Relationships with people of God will encourage us and build us up (Hebrews 10:24-25).

WORSHIP. Time spent in worship allows us to grow in our faith. It allows us to grow in our walk with the Lord. It allows us to grow closer to Him. Worship brings us into the presence of our Lord. It heightens our awareness of what it means to be in His presence (Revelation 4:8-11).

STUDY. When we study the Word of God, we become stronger Christians. When we study, we are able to distinguish between right and wrong (Hebrews 5:12-6:1). We are commanded to grow in our faith (1 Peter 2:2; 2 Peter 3:18). Failure to do so causes great concern.

SERVING OTHERS. Jesus taught us throughout His life the great need for serving others (John 13:3-9).

When we stand before God in judgment, we will be asked about our service to mankind (Matthew 25: 32-46).

The tremendous advancements in our day and the lack of focus on spiritual matters remind us of these words from the beloved Apostle Paul: "While we look not at the things which are seen, but at the things which are not seen: for the things which are seen are temporary; but the things which are not seen are eternal" (2 Corinthians 4 :16-18).

Dear God, we thank You for those things in this life that matters most. Please help us to spend our energy on these things that have redeeming value. In the Name of our Savior we pray, Amen.

Not Your Normal Happy Self

It had been one of my better weeks as far as my physical health. Please don't view this as complaining, because this isn't anything major. I have dear Christian friends who live with cancer, heart problems, and other serious illnesses every day for years.

But I was sicker than I can ever remember being. My sickness caused me to miss two appointments, and I desperately wanted to be a part of both of them.

I finally got into the doctor late on a Monday afternoon. I learned that I had strep throat and probably also had the flu. I just about completely lost my voice and had a temperature of 102. When the nurse came in to take my vital signs, she said, "It is obvious that you feel really bad, you are not your normal happy self."

I've thought a lot about her statement while sitting in my chair not feeling like doing much of anything.

There are times in the life of every child of God when we don't feel well. Some days we will not feel well physically, at times we will not feel well emotionally, and there will be times that we will not feel well spiritually. So, what do we do when we don't feel well?

REMEMBER THAT WE ARE CHILDREN OF THE KING. Just because we don't feel well doesn't mean we can lose sight of our Christianity. We still need to allow the glory of Jesus to be seen in us.

"And we all, with unveiled faces, beholding the glory of the Lord, are being transformed into the same image from one degree of glory to another" (2 Corinthians 3:18).

Those of us who preach are often called on to pray for others. We should always consider it an honor and a privilege to do so. Yet, it is good and right for us to approach God's throne when we have needs in our own lives (Hebrews 4:14-16). The Apostle Paul reminds us, "...do not be anxious about anything, but in everything by prayer and supplication with thanksgiving let your requests be made known to God" (Philippians 4:6).

REMEMBER THAT THERE ARE BETTER DAYS AHEAD. For those who are Christians, with every concern there is the hope that we will have better days ahead. If the worse happens, we can say with Paul, "For me to live is Christ, and to die is gain" (Philippians 1:21).

Paul also reminds us that whatever difficulties God's people endure in this life, they are insignificant compared to the eternal glory that shall someday be ours (2 Corinthians 4:18).

Dear Father in Heaven, we thank You for always taking care of us. We thank you for helping us get through difficult days in our lives, and we thank You for the promise of a brighter day. In the name of our Savior, who makes life possible, we pray, Amen.

"Are You Ready for Sunday?"

The memories are as fresh as if they occurred last week. Every Saturday night my mom would get our Sunday clothes ready. She would get our Sunday shoes ready (They were not expensive. We did not have much, but we had shoes that we could only wear on Sunday).

Every Saturday night mom would "check" our Sunday school lessons to make sure we had answered all the questions. Often she would ask me questions about the lessons. Getting ready for "the Lord's Day" was a big deal at our house.

Sometimes I think Sunday has just become another day of the week. All the stores are open. Many people spend Saturday nights out on the town and seemingly do very little to get ready for Sunday.

I'm just wondering, if we spent a little more time getting ready, would we enhance what happens in our churches on Sunday? May I be bold enough to make a few suggestions?

PRAY ABOUT OUR TIME TOGETHER. Pray for those who will be leading in worship. Pray for the Bible class teachers who will be teaching our children. Pray for the preacher that the sermon will be biblical and practical. Pray for those who might be considering obedience to the Lord. Pray for those who need to renew their love for Him.

To my preaching brothers, may I encourage you to pray that God will allow you to proclaim His Word with kindness and boldness. Pray that your mind might be clear and that your heart might be pure. Pray that you will be able to get yourself out of the way and present Christ. Pray the teaching of the Word might convict someone's heart. My prayer each week is, "Dear God, may the words of my mouth and the mediation of my heart be acceptable in Thy sight."

STUDY THE TEXT. Most churches these days publish in the church newsletter, or in some other form of communication, the topic and text for the Sunday sermons. It would be wonderful if every member spent some time on Saturday reading and studying the text. It would help all of us to be more informed and more prepared.

Preachers, take some time to focus your thoughts on the message you will deliver. Read through your text and your sermon notes one more time. I recently asked the venerable George Bailey if he studied on Friday and Saturday. He responded by saying, "On Friday, Saturday, Sunday morning, and during the song just before the sermon!" He added, "Of course, late in the week is not the time to start preparing, just the time to review."

PREPARE BODY, MIND, AND HEART. It would greatly enhance the worship experience if we were all better rested on Sunday morning. I know that there are extenuating circumstances (children, jobs, etc.). All too often, however, we are ill-prepared because we stayed out or up too late on Saturday night. Being rested will help our singing, it will help the study of God's Word, and it will make our worship better.

We all need to be sure that our hearts and minds are ready for worship. We should spend some time thinking about what it means to commune with our Lord (1 Corinthians 11:17-33), and what it means to edify one another (Hebrews 10:23-25). We should make sure that our hearts and minds are prepared to receive the Word.

There are other ways we can make sure we are prepared, but hopefully these will help us get started. What are other suggestions you might have that will help us get ready for Sunday?

Dear Father, please help us to give serious consideration to Your day. Help us, Father, to make sure that we have prepared ourselves as much as we possibly can. Dear God, may our worship be focused on You and not on ourselves. May we give ourselves fully to You as we worship You and give glory to our Savior. In the name of Jesus we pray, Amen.

You Just Never Know

My flight to Nashville last week presented a marvelous experience. I was on my way to Henderson for FHU Board of Trustees meetings, Lads-to-Leaders Board meetings, and to speak for the Freed Hardeman Lectures.

The young man who sat next to me on the plane was wearing his uniform. He was a member of the U.S Army. He was Airborne Special Operations Intelligence. I expressed my deep gratitude to him for his service to our country.

He talked a little about his work, but primarily about his family. We talked (actually he did most of the talking) for about an hour and a half. It was a delightful experience.

I asked him what he was going to do after he retired. He said, "I'm working on another project, do you mind if I tell you about it?" I told him I would love to hear about it.

He said that he wanted to be a Chaplain. He had completed his undergraduate work and that he now has to start his graduate studies. I asked him if he had selected a graduate school. He said no.

I was able to talk to him about the possibility of attending Freed Hardeman. I also had the opportunity to tell him about a friend of mine who preaches for the church of Christ in the town where he is stationed. I assured him that he along with his young family would be welcomed.

It was also wonderful to be able to talk to him about Jesus. Isn't it wonderful to be able to talk about Jesus? My experience made me think about how important it is for us to always be ready to talk about Christ and His Word (1 Peter 3:15). It reminded me that we never know about how our interactions with others might influence the direction of their life and more importantly their eternity. You just never know.

YOU NEVER KNOW WHEN YOUR EXAMPLE MIGHT INFLUENCE SOMEONE ELSE TO FOLLOW JESUS. Paul instructed Timothy with these words, "Let no one look down on your youthfulness, but rather in speech, conduct, love, faith and purity, show yourself an example of those who believe (1 Timothy 4:12). Our influence can be a powerful tool to win others to Jesus (1 Peter 3:1-8).

YOU NEVER KNOW WHEN YOU MIGHT HAVE AN OPPORTUNITY TO PROCLAIM THE WORD OF GOD. Paul said, "...For my part, I am eager to preach the gospel to you also who are in Rome." The phrase that he uses here means literally, "I am on fire" to preach the Gospel. We are reminded of the great prophet of God Jeremiah when he was arrested for preaching (Jeremiah 20:9-10).

We should always be ready to share the Good News with others. We should always be ready to give an answer for the hope that is within us (1 Peter 3:15).

YOU NEVER KNOW WHEN YOU MIGHT HAVE AN OPPORTUNITY TO BRING JOY TO OTHERS. This wonderful young man was so excited to tell me about his desire to be a chaplain. He was also extremely happy to learn that I might be able to be of help to him in some way.

We find some of our greatest joy in being of service to people around us. The Word of God tells us that we should rejoice when others rejoice. What a rich blessing God has given us when we can share His Word with others.

Dear Father, please help us keep our eyes open for opportunities to talk to people about Jesus. Help us dear God to always be ready. Help us to live in such a way that people will want to hear what we have to say. Thank you, Lord for your precious Word that can penetrate the hearts of those who hear. In the Name of our Savior we pray, Amen.

Stir What You Got!

One of the highlights of my life is my weekly lunch with my dear friend, Steve Bailey, who is the outstanding preacher for the church in Waxahachie.

Occasionally we will try something new, but we pretty much have our normal haunts. Sometimes we eat down at Dunston's where we run into Lee Roy Jordan. Sometimes we meet down at the West End and eat at Haufbrau's. Most of the time we eat Mexican food.

Our topics of conversation pretty much run the gambit. We always talk about our families. We discuss our disgust with Jerry Jones and the 'Boys. We talk about our work, our upcoming trip to Israel, and sermons.

Steve is as fine a minister and as fine a man as I have ever known.

Well, at this week's lunch, Steve told me a great story, and I asked him if he would mind me sharing it. He said he would be fine with it. First the story and then some application.

There was a man who was driving home late at night from a brief trip. He stopped at a roadside diner in a Texas hill country town to snag a quick cup of coffee. As is typical of many people, he quickly used all the sugar packets the waitress had left on the table for him, but he wanted more.

As the waitress came near his table again, he called out, "I want some more sugar, please." The crusty old gal defiantly put her hands on her hips, leaned over toward him and snapped, "Stir what you got!"

Isn't that a great story? It seems that there are a couple of different approaches we can take to life. We can either sit around and complain about what we don't have, or we can take what we do have and make the most of it.

Do you ever wonder why you don't have more talents/gifts to serve God? Stir what you got—you just might recognize you already have way more than you really need (Matthew 24:14-30)!

Do you ever wonder why you don't have more friends to encourage you? Stir what you got! If you are a part of the church, you have many friends who care about you. Most important of all is the Friend who gave His life for you (John 15:13).

Do you ever wonder if you are blessed? Stir what you got! As children of God we have more blessings than we can imagine (James 1:17; Ephesians 1:3).

Do you ever wonder if anyone is listening to you? Stir what you got! Our Father in Heaven promises us that we can come before His throne at any time, and He will hear our prayers (Hebrews 4:14-16).

Do you ever wonder if you are loved? Stir what you got! "'For God so loved the world, that He gave His only begotten Son, that whoever believes in Him shall not perish, but have eternal life" (John 3:16).

May God help all of us to remember how blessed we are. Don't sit around wondering why you don't have more. Get busy in the work of the Lord, and STIR WHAT YOU GOT!

Dear Father in Heaven, we thank You for all You have done for us. We thank You for the tremendous ways You continually bless our lives. Help us, dear God, not to focus on what we don't have, but to keep our minds on how blessed we are because of Jesus. It is in His powerful name we pray, Amen.

The Land of the Living

Two requests, neither of which is uncommon, have been made of me in recent weeks. The first one was when one of our teen girls came to me and asked if I would marry her. Of course, I told her that I could not because I am very happily married! I then told her that it would be a privilege to perform her wedding ceremony. All that she needs to do now is find the right man to join her on her wedding day! :)

The other request came from one of our "senior" members who requested that I preach his funeral. He is a wonderful man of God, and it will be an honor to fulfill this request.

In our culture, we view marriage as a new beginning. We consider this happy time, when a man and woman come together to build a new home and a new life, as one of the most joyful times in life. We are right to look at marriage in this way.

At the opposite end of the spectrum, in our culture we view death as the end of a life. We talk about "end of life" issues and "the last days" of an individual's life. We often consider it to be an extremely sorrowful time.

It seems as though I've been attending more funerals than normal lately. My preacher friends will understand this. The longer you work with a particular church and the more you get to know the members and their extended families, the more you are called on to help with funerals.

I recently heard a preacher say something that I had heard years ago, but had forgotten. I believe his statement is biblically correct. He said of the departed loved one, "He has left the land of the dying to go to the land of the living!" What a wonderful thought.

As we grow older, our bodies begin to wear out (2 Corinthians 4:16-5:4, see also Ecclesiastes 12:1-8). However, as you know, we don't just learn this from scripture, we learn it from the personal experiences of our lives.

Unless Jesus returns first, every living person will die (Hebrews 9:27). This present world truly is the land of the dying!

However, when this body decays and returns to the dust of the ground, the "spirit returns to God who gave it" (Ecclesiastes 12:7). In Heaven, our spirit, the person who we really are, will dwell forever in the land of the living!

In the land of the living, "...there will no longer be any death; there will no longer be any mourning, or crying, or pain: the first things have passed away" (Revelation 21:4).

In the land of the living we will join with all the saints to praise our Savior forever (Revelation 4:8-11). In the land of the living we will have, "...no need of the sun or of the moon to shine...for the glory of God has illumined...and its lamp is the Lamb" (Revelation 21:23).

In the land of the dying we are strangers and pilgrims searching for a better country, a heavenly one (Hebrews 11:13-16), a land where we will live forever. It is the land of the living where our Savior went to prepare a home for us (John 14:1-3).

Dear Father in Heaven, we give You thanks for the promise and hope that we have for a better place. We long to spend eternity in Your presence, in the presence of our Savior, and in the presence of those who have gone on before us. Dear God, help us to live in this land of the dying in such a way that someday we will be called to be forever in the land of the living. In the name of Jesus we pray, Amen.

Eating with Impunity

While watching the late news the other night, we saw one of those world class chefs being interviewed about the different kinds of foods people eat on Super Bowl Sunday. By the way, did you know that more food is eaten by Americans on Super Bowl Sunday than any other day of the year other than Thanksgiving? How's that for a free fun fact? That also reminds me of another interesting fact I learned recently from a friend of mine. Did you know that the average time that plays are actually in progress during a football game (which in the case of the Super Bowl will last more than four hours) is eleven (yes, you read that right) eleven minutes! Astonishing! However, that last little tidbit of information has nothing to do with the words I am writing.

So, back to the chef. At one point during the interview he was talking about how much he loves to eat. He made the statement, "My one goal in life is to eat with impunity."

I started thinking about that statement and how I had never heard of or thought of the idea of impunity associated with eating. I pulled up dictionary.com (you know, the modern-day Webster's) to make sure I was right about what impunity means. It told me that impunity comes from a Latin word meaning to be exempt from punishment or immune from detrimental effects. Now wouldn't that be super? To be able to spend your life eating without any detrimental effects. In our day, it seems that this is impossible. It seems that there are some detrimental effects tied to everything we eat (at least those things that we really enjoy eating)!

While that may be a worthy physical goal, albeit a very difficult (if not impossible) one to achieve, there is something we can do in this life without impunity. We can make decisions and choices that will exempt us from punishment. We can choose to follow Jesus in everything we do, and we will not be punished, but rather ultimately we will be rewarded.

When we are in Christ we receive the righteousness of God (2 Corinthians 5:21). That is what it means to live life with impunity. Paul also declares that for those who are in Christ there is no condemnation (Romans 8:1). That's what it means to live life with impunity. Does it mean, as some would have us to believe, that we will never sin again? No, John reminds Christians that if we claim that we have no sin we are only deceiving ourselves (1 John 1:8). We will continue to sin, however "if we confess our sin, He is faithful and righteous to forgive us" (1 John 1:9). It is when we are walking in the light that His blood cleanses us (1 John 1:7). That is what it means to live life with impunity.

There are too many Christians who, although they are walking in the light and are continually being cleansed by the blood of Jesus, are still living a life of guilt. They are wondering if they are lost or saved. An old preacher in Alabama used to say living the Christian life is not like being on a yo-yo. We are not lost one minute and saved the next. Jesus came to bring us the abundant life (John 10:10). When we walk with Him we can live that abundant life with impunity, and we can know that eternal salvation is ours (1 John 5:13).

Dear God, help us to know that if we are walking with the Savior, we can live an abundant life with impunity. Father, help us to know that we have an assured entrance into the eternal home of the soul, where there is rest, sweet rest. Thank You for saving us and allowing us to partake of Your righteousness. In your Son's precious name we pray, Amen.

Immersed in the Word

A Christian sister who has two PhDs and has taught on the collegiate level wrote these words about a preacher friend of hers: "He stands as a beacon to those who are looking for truth to come from the pulpit. If one is immersed in the Word, accepting its authentic origin and message, one will not be arrogant and dismissive of its doctrines. True study—not critical analysis—humbles the reader of the Bible."

While I do not agree with everything John MacArthur writes, much of what he says is very thought-provoking. Such are these words he recently penned: "Those who take God's Word seriously spend many hours in study. Coming out of diligent study are lessons, sermons, articles, and books that are deep, weighty, sober, doctrinally coherent, and theologically consistent. Sadly, today's evangelicals aren't known for being profound, sober-minded, or consistent; instead they've developed a reputation for being superficial, trivial, doctrinally erratic, and theologically naïve. Want proof? Walk into your local Christian bookstore, sample the preaching online, survey the blogs—the shoe fits. So, if the way back is to fear God, honor His Word, and work hard to understand and teach it accurately, what kinds of things are standing in the way?"

To answer that question two primary passages come to mind. The first is 2 Timothy 4. Every preacher is commanded to "preach the Word." This is a solemn charge. We are to be serious about preaching God's Word. Some have seemingly turned the preaching of God's Word into something akin to a circus side show.

Every time I stand before an audience to proclaim God's Word this verse strikes me with a holy fear. I will someday stand before the Judge of the universe and give an account of how I handled His Word. We are to be instant in season and out of season. This statement simply means we are to preach the Word all the time.

The other passage that immediately comes to my mind is Hebrews 4:12. This verse gives us the characteristics of the Word of God. The Word of God is precise and accurate. We need preachers of God's Word who are skilled in handling the Word. They should be skilled in the reading, interpretation and exposition of His Word. The faithful preacher must spend many hours in study and in prayer to rightly divide the word of truth.

There can be no substitute for this study. I remember as a young preacher hearing about brother Gus Nichols studying the Word for four hours every morning, long before most people were up and around. Brother Franklin Camp, who was one of the great students of the Old Testament in the previous generation, stated that if Brother Nichols needed to study four hours then he would need to study five hours each morning. And this he did! There is no room for laziness. We cannot be infatuated with the culture. The Apostle Paul stated that he was more concerned with what the Lord thought about his teaching than what others thought (1 Corinthians 4:3).

May God help those of us who preach to have the time we so desperately need to study every day. There has been a famine in the land when it comes to the study of the Word. Those of us who stand and proclaim God's Word must lead the way. If we do not study, neither will those who hear us.

If you are an elder in the church, demand that your preacher gives proper attention to study. Make it possible for him to have the time he needs. Brother George Bailey tells about a congregation who rented a room in a local hotel so that he could get away from the office every day to study.

If you are a member of a church who has a preacher who proclaims the whole counsel of God, pray for him, encourage him, and give him the time he needs to prepare sermons that will help the church grow spiritually as well as numerically.

Dear God, in a day when Your Word is not held in high esteem, we pray that You will help those of us who preach, as well as those of us who listen, to immerse ourselves in Your Word. Help those of us who preach to stand as beacons for those who are looking for Truth to come from the pulpit. Father, help all of us to grow in our faith and in the knowledge of Your Word. In Jesus' holy name we pray, Amen.

The People Are Suffering

While watching the late news one night several years ago we saw a young man being interviewed about the NBC Late Night television fiasco. If you watched any news during those days or read any articles there was something about the Jay Leno/Conan O'Brien late night wars. They asked this young man what he thought about the situation and he responded by saying something like, "They need to get on with it, because the fans, the people are suffering." I thought, you have got to be kidding! "The people are suffering???" Have we become so inane that we believe suffering occurs because of some television wars? Isn't it amazing what we call suffering in our day?

There are many people in our world who are suffering, but suffering is not enduring the "late night wars." The people who have lost loved ones and everything they own in Haiti are suffering. The people in our world who will not have a meal today or tomorrow are suffering. The family who lost their only son in war is suffering. The Christian family who lost their child in a car accident is suffering. The woman whose husband walked out on her for someone else and left her to raise the children by herself is suffering. The man who lost his job after many years of committed service to the company is suffering. The family whose child has forsaken the Lord and everything that they were taught is suffering. The preacher who was "let go," because the church needed a younger man, is suffering. The church that has been divided because some member felt that their way was more important than "His Way" is suffering. The teen who lives for God and is ridiculed and isolated while others follow the way of the world is suffering.

If we suffer because of our faith, we will be blessed. If we suffer we are in good company. Our Savior suffered for us (Luke 24:46; 1 Peter 2:21). He told us that in this world we would have tribulation (John 16:13). He reminds us that if we "suffer with Him," we will also be "glorified with Him" (Romans 8:17). He also told us to remember that we should not find it strange that we suffer, because if the Master suffers persecution, the servants will also suffer persecution (John 15:20). Suffering can make us stronger if it is handled correctly (James 1:2-3).

It isn't that people do not or will not suffer. It's just that we confuse what we sometimes believe to be suffering with real suffering. We will all face some suffering in our lives. If you are suffering today, may God give you the strength to endure. Above all things, remember these words from the Apostle Paul, "For momentary, light affliction is producing for us an eternal weight of glory far beyond all comparison" (2 Corinthians 4:17).

Dear God, please help us understand that so much of what masquerades as suffering is not real. Help us to pray for and encourage those around us who are truly suffering. Help us to endure the suffering that is a part of our lives with faithfulness so that someday we can live forever with the One who suffered for us. It is in His name we pray, Amen.

A Late Night Prayer

As I type these words I'm on a plane somewhere between Atlanta and Dallas. It is late. By the time I get home tonight, it will be after midnight. I'm tired. It's been a long couple of days. We were in board meetings all day today at Freed Hardeman. They were great meetings and, once again, it was a reminder of many of the reasons why we love FHU so much.

It's been an extremely busy month, and we're just getting started. While we were taking off tonight from Atlanta, I felt a little sorry for myself. I closed my eyes for just a minute, said a prayer (primarily for my family), then it hit me: "Jeff, who are you kidding? You ought to be ashamed of yourself. Here you are flying on a plane (that has Wi-Fi, wahoo!). You will get in your nice, comfortable car (if I can find my keys when we land), drive home to a warm house, and crawl in a very warm comfortable bed with the woman you love more than life. You will have dinner tomorrow night with friends, and worship Sunday with some of God's greatest people!"

There are hundreds of thousands of people in Haiti tonight who will not get into a vehicle, because they don't have one. They will not walk into a house tonight, because their house is gone. They will not sleep in a bed tonight. If they even get to eat a meal tomorrow, they will do so without friends and family, because they lost them in this terrible disaster. As you know, hundreds of thousands of Haitians have lost loved ones, lost homes, and everything they own. Our hearts ache for those who are suffering tonight. God's Word teaches that we are to "weep with those who weep" (Romans 12:15). He also instructs us to bear the burdens of our brothers and sisters who are troubled (Galatians 6:1-2).

It is encouraging to know that so many people around the world are coming to the aid of the people of Haiti. It is encouraging to know that so many Christians and churches are joining in to bring relief. I know there are hundreds of churches across this land who are involved in helping in some way.

 By the way, if you are reading this and you are looking for a place to help, or if you just want to learn about some of the good that is being done, allow me to encourage you to look at Brotherhood News at the address: *brotherhoodnews.com*. Randal Matheny and his crew have done a tremendous job compiling and highlighting some of the work that is being done.

Maybe you have yet to help but would like to do so. If you know of other works that are being carried out to help the people of Haiti, please feel free to let us know, and we will pass it along.

I am going to say another prayer before I land.

"Dear Father, please forgive me for being self-centered. Please help all of us to do a better job of following the example of our Savior who was always looking for ways to serve others. Father, help us to find ways to reach out to those who are suffering. Please, dear God, be with the people of Haiti who are hurting tonight, as well as others around the world who are suffering. Help Your people be the hands, feet, mouth, and heart of Jesus." In His compassionate name we pray, Amen.

Can't Get the Hang of It

Some of our dearest friends have two precious grandchildren. During a recent visit to see them, Maw-Maw was talking to the oldest child and, as is often the case, he was entertaining. He said of his younger brother, "Maw-Maw, he just cannot get the hang of responsibility!" This would be quite humorous. However, it is all the more so when you realize that older brother just turned five and little brother (the one who can't get the hang of responsibility) is 16 months! I have laughed until I've cried on that one! One reason I enjoy this story so much is that I know that both of these boys are going to "get the hang of responsibility." They have wonderful Christian parents and grandparents who will train them in the admonition of the Lord.

This little serendipity has caused me to think about how sad it is that there are so many adults who just cannot seem to get the hang of responsibility:

Men who cannot get the hang of responsibility when it comes to being the spiritual leaders in the family.

Women who cannot get the hang of responsibility when it comes to being the helper God wants them to be.

Parents who cannot get the hang of responsibility when it comes to training children in the nurture and the admonition of the Lord.

Parents who cannot get the hang of responsibility when it comes to living their faith as a model for their children.

Parents who cannot get the hang of responsibility when it comes to teaching their children the Word of God, rather than thinking that it's the job of the youth minister, Bible class teachers, preachers, elders, etc.

Elders who cannot get the hang of responsibility when it comes to shepherding the flock of God, rather than serving as a board.

Elders who cannot get the hang of responsibility when it comes to making certain that Truth is taught in the pulpit and in Bible classes.

Deacons who cannot get the hang of responsibility when it comes to fulfilling their obligation to be active, faithful servants.

Preachers who cannot get the hang of responsibility when it comes to preaching the Truth in love.

Preachers who cannot get the hang of responsibility when it comes to fulfilling the work of a minister.

Christians who cannot get the hang of responsibility when it comes to seeking first the Kingdom of God in everything we do.

Christians who cannot get the hang of responsibility when it comes to sharing the Good News with family, friends, coworkers, classmates, and teammates.

Dear Father, please help us get the hang of responsibility and be the kind of people You want us to be. In Jesus' name we pray, Amen.

Anonymous

This is something I've been thinking about for a while, and I've tried to save it just for the right moment. Well, the right moment is here, and it probably has nothing to do with the fact that we are just a few hours from the National Championship game between Alabama & Texas! I happen to be from Alabama, but I now live in Texas. We love Texas for many reasons, but I am a huge fan of the Crimson Tide. I have been all my life. In our wonderful congregation we have approximately six people (as far as I know) who claim to be from Alabama. Three of us are fans of the Crimson Tide and the other three are fans of that "other" team from Alabama. :) While there are fans from various schools/teams around the nation most of our folks are fans of Texas, Oklahoma, Texas A&M, and Texas Tech. There is much to like about the Longhorns this year. They have an excellent coaching staff, they have outstanding players (including some wonderful young men who are Christians), and they play an exciting brand of football. I've tried (with the emphasis on tried) not to say too much about the game for fear that my team would lose, and I would have to eat a lot of crow! So, this is all pretty exciting, and I hope the team from T-Town will put it on the team in burnt orange.

Having said all of that, these thoughts were not intended to be about a football game. They are meant to be about an anonymous gift I received. One of my favorite gifts of all time! Now, through the years I have receive many anonymous "gifts." There have been unsigned letters from people that did not like something that was said in a sermon or who were angry about some decision made by the church. For many years, every January I received an envelope with no return address that contained a one-page flyer about a special seminar that would help you become a better public speaker. It was never signed, but it came like clockwork every year.

This gift is different. The helmet is an authentic Crimson Tide helmet autographed by Gene Stallings, who happened to be the last coach that took Alabama to a national championship. It was auctioned off at a benefit dinner that we attended several weeks ago. While I don't know the exact amount, I do know that it was sold for a rather large sum of money. I have no idea who bought it and gave it to me. I am deeply thankful not only for the gift, but also for the very kind note that was attached to it when it was placed on my desk. The money went to a wonderful cause (the training of young men to preach the Gospel). Part of me wishes I knew who gave me this wonderful gift so that I could express proper appreciation. Another part of me is thankful that the anonymous giver can enjoy knowing that they made this preacher a very happy man. So, if you are reading this, thank you, thank you, thank you. I will cherish this wonderful gift for many years to come.

My life has been blessed by knowing many givers. The kind of givers that Jesus speaks of in Matthew 25 who will give a cup of cold water in His name. The kind of givers like the widow in Luke 21 who Jesus holds up before us as a model giver. The kind of givers like the Macedonian Christians who gave beyond their ability (2 Corinthians 8). The kind of givers who give in secret, and their gifts are known only by the Father. (Matthew 6:1-4) These are the kind of people who have learned from the greatest Giver of all (John 3:16; Romans 5:8). These are the givers who make our world a better place.

Thank you, Father, for people who have learned how to give from You. Thank You for people who give unselfishly of their time, their money, their talents, and their lives. Thank You, most of all, for giving us the greatest gift ever given! Help us all to learn to give like You. In Jesus' name we pray, Amen.

Everybody's a Role Model

When I was a child playing little league football, it seemed like every boy who played the game had to have a haircut just like Johnny U. Now, if you can remember that, you are showing your age. As a boy, I wanted that Johnny U haircut, but I wanted to be able to throw like Joe Willie. All my life I have watched individuals look up to professional athletes as role-models. In recent years, we have heard some of them proclaim boldly that they will not be role-models, and no one should look up to them. I can only say, "Are you kidding us?" You think you can be paid millions of dollars, have your image splashed across every TV in America, and not have young boys want to be just like you? The same is true with singers, movie stars, and a host of other famous people in our country.

Steve Farrar in his book, Anchor Man, tells a story from the life of Tommy Bolt—known years ago on the PGA tour for his elegant swing and his nasty temper.

"Bolt was conducting a golf clinic one afternoon for a group of businesspeople. Bolt was showing them how easy the mechanics of the swing were and, to demonstrate, he turned to his teenage son and said, 'Son, imitate what I do for this gentleman.' His son immediately took his nine-iron and threw it into the lake." We can only hope that there are not too many young men who will demonstrate the recent antics of some professional athletes.

The reality is that the rich and famous are not the only ones who are being watched. The truth is we are all role-models. Someone is watching every one of us. Some young person wants to be just like you. Parents, if we have young children or even teenagers in our home their ears are like recorders. They hear everything we say and will repeat some of it. They watch everything we do, and many of them want to be like us. Preachers, there are young men who are looking up to us to see if how we live matches what we say. They want to know if our walk matches our talk. Teenagers, there are younger children who idolize you, they watch everything you do, and they want to be just like you. The Apostle Paul says in 1 Timothy 4:12, "Let no one look down on your youthfulness, but rather in speech, conduct, love, faith and purity, show yourself an example of those who believe." We should always remember Paul's words in 1 Corinthians 11:1, "Be imitators of me, just as I also am of Christ."

May God help all of us to be conscious of the fact that we are all role-models. May we live our lives to bring glory to Him and to encourage those around us. Can you think of some ways you can be better role-models in the New Year?

Dear Father, help us to realize that no matter who we are, someone is watching us. Help us to imitate You so that we can lead others to Christ. In His name we pray, Amen.

A Lifetime of Lessons

It was on Christmas Eve when we buried our mother. It seems like it was just yesterday when we were driving to her house to celebrate Christmas with the whole family. Mom loved Christmas! She went all out with the decorations, bought way too many gifts for her children and grandchildren, and cooked an outstanding Christmas meal (we always had her famous "Watergate" salad, a strawberry cake that still makes my mouth water, and no casseroles!) She always wanted to load the family up and go look at Christmas lights, and generally she just wanted the family to be together. I will never go through another Christmas without thinking about her.

I realize that I am not the only one who has difficulty during the holidays because of the loss of someone who is dear. I know that some of you who are reading this will go through the holidays without someone you love for the first time this year. Please know that you will be in our thoughts and prayers.

Thinking about my mom early this morning reminded me of some of the most important lessons she taught me during her life.

First, Mom taught me to love and support my mate. She loved my dad deeply, and she was always supportive of the work he was doing for the Lord. The few times I can remember Mom being visibly angry was when she felt someone had wronged my dad. She stood faithfully beside him for 50 years. She was always there for him in every aspect of his work.

Mom taught me to love my children. Her love for her children was unconditional. From our days in youth sports until we graduated from high school, Mom was at every school function, athletic event and church activity that involved her children. Mom was not a well-known teacher, but she took the time to teach her children. She taught us the Word of God from our earliest days.

Mom taught me to love the Lord. I am convinced that one of the biggest reasons I am preaching today is because of the influence of my mom. She loved the Lord and His church. She taught us to put church above everything else. We would never miss the worship of the church to play in a ball game. I can remember being pulled out of games and practices to make it to midweek Bible study on time. We would sometimes go to church in our uniform and leave after church to make it to part of a game. Mom instilled in us a commitment to the Lord that continues to strengthen my life today.

Mom taught me to love life. She saw the good in others and had a beautiful forgiving spirit that permeated her life. I remember my mom being a happy person. I know that she had cares and concerns, however, she never allowed them to burden her life.

I will always cherish the memories of my mom, especially at Christmas. I thank God for the influence she had and continues to have on my life. I will forever hold these memories close to my heart. What lessons do you remember from a loved one who is not with you during this holiday season?

Dear Father, on this Christmas Eve we give You thanks for the lessons we have learned from those who have gone on before us. Please help us to take these lessons and pass them on to others. Father, help us to show Your love to those who are still with us. In Your Son's name we pray, Amen.

A Beige Life

Two of my dear friends were talking recently, and during their conversation, they begin talking about our friendship. One of them said of me, "Before he knew us, his life was beige!" While I may not agree that my life was beige before I met these two, I have to admit that they have brought much more color into my life than I previously had.

This conversation got me to thinking about how many Christians I know who appear to live beige, drab, boring lives. There will certainly be days in every person's life where we will not be on top of the world. However, if there is anyone who should live a joyful, colorful life, it should be those who have been redeemed by the precious blood of Jesus. Jesus himself said that He came into the world so we could enjoy abundant lives (John 10:10). The word for abundant in this passage is the Greek word, "perissos." It carries with it the idea of something that is superior, extraordinary, over and above, superadded. It was this knowledge that caused Paul to say, "Rejoice in the Lord always" (Philippians 4:4).

When Christians live joyful lives, we spread the beauty of the Good News to everyone around us. There is an interesting statement in Ephesians 3:9-11 where Paul says that we are to make known the "manifold" wisdom of God. The Greek word for "manifold," is the word "polypoikilos." It is a word that denotes being marked with a great variety of colors. A Christian who lives a "beige" life will never show a drab, boring world what real, abundant living is all about. We should be, "the sweet aroma of the knowledge of Him in every place" (2 Corinthians 2:14). When "Christ is formed" (Galatians 4:19) in us, we will live joyful, colorful lives, and the world will see Jesus (John 12:21).

Dear Father, help us live our lives in such a way that those around us will not ever think that the Christian life is a "beige" life. Help us live the abundant life that Jesus brings us so that our family and friends will want to know about the unsearchable riches of Christ. In His glorious name we pray, Amen.

I Ain't Gonna Do It

Some of you who read this will know the man who told this story, so I decided not to call any names. As the story goes, when this dear brother (who is quite advanced in years now) was a boy, his father had given him and his brother some instructions. Our friend followed dad's instructions just as a boy should, but his brother's response was, "I ain't gonna do it." Needless to say, their dad was quite incensed at the reaction, and the son paid the proper penalty.

A few of us who have heard the story have taken it upon ourselves to allow this phrase to live in perpetuity, and a long time as well :). When there is something we don't like or we are reticent about, we just repeat, "I ain't gonna do it."

I've thought a lot about how that statement represents a selfishness all balled up in somebody's heart. It says I am too good, or I just don't like what you've told me to do. It is a stubborn rebelliousness that defies authority.

Most parents would not allow their children to get away with saying it, but is it possible that we could display the same attitude that is revealed in the statement?

God says, "Love your neighbor as yourself," and we say, "I ain't gonna do it."

He says that we must be baptized to be saved, and we say, "I ain't gonna do it."

He says, "Take up your cross daily," and we say, "I ain't gonna do it."

He says that we should forgive one another, and we say, "I ain't gonna do it."

He says, "Bear one another's burdens," and we say, "I ain't gonna do it."

He says, "Be kind to one another," and we say, "I ain't gonna do it."

He says, "Visit the fatherless and widows," but we say, "I ain't gonna do it."

He says, "Pray for your leaders," but we say, "I ain't gonna do it."

He says, "Love the brotherhood," but we say, "I ain't gonna do it."

He says, "Pray for one another," but we say, "I ain't gonna do it."

He says, "Encourage one another by worshipping regularly together," but we say, "I ain't gonna do it."

He says, "Speak words that edify and build up," but we say, "I ain't gonna do it."

He says, "Obey those that have the rule over you," but we say, "I ain't gonna do it."

He says, "If you love me, keep my commandments," but we say, "I ain't gonna do it."

One day we are going to stand before the judgment seat of God and expect Him to let us into His Heaven. For all of those who have spent their lives saying, "I ain't gonna do it," and who still demand Heaven, I wonder what He will say???

Dear God, help us to have a heart that says we will seek to do everything you have commanded us to do. Help us to show our love to You by making Your Will the center of all that we do. In Jesus Name, Amen.

May I Help You?

Laura and I visited a wonderful Christian sister in the hospital the other day. As we were leaving the hospital, we were stopped at an extremely busy intersection. While sitting there we noticed a car stopped in the middle of the road on the other side of the highway. We could see an elderly lady in the car, and she had her head bowed down. We decided to try to help, so I jumped out of the car. Laura crawled over to the driver's side and went down the street to turn around. When I got out of the car, it started raining. I waited for traffic to clear up and walked over to her car. I tapped on her window and said, "Ma'am, are you alright? Is there any way I can help you?" She rolled the window down and said, "No thank you, I'm just waiting for someone to come out of the IHOP across the street. But thank you very much, and God bless you." I said, "Ma'am, maybe you should pull out of the middle of the road into the parking lot." She said, "Oh, thank you, that's a good idea!"

To say the least, I was not thrilled about standing in the rain as I waited for Laura to find a convenient place to turn around. However, if we would have continued driving and not stopped to help, I would have felt bad. Next time I see a stalled car with a little old lady I will stop again, even if nothing is wrong.

In our world, it is so easy to refuse to help others. It is easy to keep driving. It is easy to walk by on the other side of the road. (Luke 10) However, if we want to be true servants of Christ, we must be willing to stop and help others. Jesus often stopped along the way to help others. He showed us the true meaning of service when He washed His disciples' feet (John 13).

We have opportunities every day to show Jesus to people in the world around us. We are the eyes of Jesus to look for those who are hurting. We are the arms of Jesus to reach out to the downtrodden. We are the hands of Jesus to lift up those who have fallen. We are the feet of Jesus to take the Gospel to those who have not heard.

We must be willing to help others in a physical way, just as our Savior did (Matthew 11:5). Luke reports to us that Jesus went everywhere doing good for others (Acts 10:38). As His disciples, we also should do good for as many as we can, as often as we can, as much as we can. But let us never forget that the primary purpose for Christ coming to the earth was to seek and save all of us who were lost (Luke 19:10). In our doing good for others, let's be certain that we do not forget to tell them about the Lamb of God who takes away the sins of the world (John 1:29).

Dear God, help us to reach out to others and do as much good as we can. Please help us to have the mind and heart of Jesus. Help us tell as many people as possible the Good News that Jesus takes away sins. In the name of Jesus we pray, Amen.

Stick to What You Know, Pops

Whenever my granddaughter gets hurt, if I'm around I'll say to her, "Come to Dr. Pop's operating room and let me do some surgery." It almost always makes her start laughing, even if she is crying.

One day out of the clear blue after hurting herself and after I said, "Come to Dr. Pops...," she said, "Stick to what you know pops, stick to what you know!" I said, "What do you mean, stick to what you know?"

She responded by saying, "Pops you're not a Doctor, you are a preacher!" It was encouraging that she understands that her Pops doesn't know anything about being a Doctor, but he knows at least something about being a preacher.

That's good Theology, coming from a four year old. There are too many of us who spend our time trying to involve ourselves in matters we don't know about. We should all stick to what we know. There are some things all of us can know.

We can know that God loves us (John 3:16).

We can know that God loves us, even while we are sinners (Romans 5:8).

We can know that we can't save ourselves (Jeremiah 10:23).

We can know that we can only be redeemed by the blood of Jesus (2 Corinthians 5:21; 1 Peter 1:18-19).

We can know that God's Grace is available to everyone (Titus 2:10), and that He wants everyone to be saved (2 Peter 3:9).

We can know that we must put our faith is Jesus (John 8:24).

We can know that we must repent (Luke 13:3).

We can know that we must confess our faith in Christ (Romans 10:10).

We can know that we must be immersed into Christ to receive forgiveness of our sins (Acts 2:38; Acts 22:16).

We can know that we must remain faithful to our Lord as long as we live (Revelation 2:10).

We can know that God will not allow us to be tempted more than we are capable of handling, and that He will always provide for us a way to escape (1 Corinthians 10:13).

We can know that all things work together for our good if we love the Lord (Romans 8:28).

We can know that if we keep walking in the light, His blood continually cleanses our sins (1 John 1:7).

We can know that God has given us everything we need for this life (2 Peter 1:3).

We can know that our God cares deeply about us (1 Peter 5:7).

We can know that our Lord has prepared a glorious place for us in Heaven (John 14:1-3).

We can know that Eternal life is ours (1 John 5:13).

We can know that our loving Father hears our prayers (Hebrews 4:12-14).

Dear Father in Heaven, Please help us to depend more on You, than we do ourselves. Help us to focus on what we can know and not trouble ourselves with what we don't know. Thank you for the knowledge You have provided to us in Your Word. In the Name of Jesus we pray, Amen.

Other titles available from The Jenkins Institute:

The Living Word: Sermons of Jerry A. Jenkins
The Glory of Preaching
Before I Go: Notes from Older Preachers

Thoughts from the Mound
All I Ever Wanted to Do Was Preach
I Hope You Have to Pinch Yourself
Don't Quit on a Monday

Five Secrets and a Decision
Centered: Marking Your Map in a Muddled World
Me, You, and the People in the Pews
From Mother's Day to Father's Day

A Minister's Heart
A Youth Minister's Heart
A Mother's Heart
A Father's Heart

Free Evangelism Resources by Jerry Jenkins:
God Speaks Today
Lovingly Leading Men to the Savior

To order, visit thejenkinsinstitute.com/shop